E=MC³: Entrepreneurs' Theory of Relativity

Abhijit Chatterjee

walnutpublication
.com
INDIA • UK • USA

Paperback ISBN: 979-8-89171-140-2

eBook ISBN: 979-8-89171-141-9

First Published on September, 2024

Published by Walnut Publication

(an imprint of Vyusta Ventures LLP)

www.walnutpublication.com

India

#625, 6th Floor, Nexus Esplanade, Rasulgarh, Bhubaneswar

Unit# 909, 9th Floor, Wave Silver Tower, Sector-18, Noida - 201301

USA

1820 Avenue M #849, Brooklyn, NY 11230, United States of America

Distributed by

Promoting the spirit of entrepreneurship nurtured under NEP 2020 - igniting innovation, empowering minds, and shaping tomorrow's visionary leaders.

धर्मेन्द्र प्रधान
धर्मेन्द्र प्रधान
Dharmendra Pradhan

शिक्षा मंत्री
भारत सरकार
Minister of Education
Government of India

Foreword

I am happy to know that a book titled "E=MC^3: Entrepreneurs Theory of Relativity" by Abhijit Chatterjee is being brought out for release at the prestigious Oxford University, UK. My greetings to the entrepreneur-author on this occasion.

The book delves into a theory of relativity for entrepreneurs, encapsulating in the equation "E=MC^3" - where 'E' stands for the Entrepreneur, 'M' stands for Management, and the three 'Cs' represent Capacity, Collaboration and Capital. This theory emanating from the real-life experiences of the author forms the foundation of the book and underscores the interconnectedness of these key components in the journey of entrepreneurship. The book is both 'rooted' in the essence of ancient wisdom and 'futuristic' in terms of modern entrepreneurial dynamics which highlight the importance of entrepreneurship and education in shaping India's future.

Entrepreneurship is a dynamically evolving domain with no fixed doctrine to determine its success. Entrepreneurs of varying interests have devised their own ingenious ways to script success in their ventures. An entrepreneur may have her own model and approach to business but to succeed, she must focus on the basic managerial dynamics as outlined by the author in form of '3 Cs' - Capacity, Collaboration and Capital. I would like to add one more 'C' - Conviction as an irreducible minimum for the success of any entrepreneurial venture that has built-in risk propensity.

Abhijit Chatterjee has enriched the content of the book from his personal entrepreneurial journey and I am sure, the new budding entrepreneurs who are usually gripped by fear of failure will overcome it by following the nuggets shared by the author. I take this opportunity to congratulate the author for this inspiring publication. The growing tribe of new entrepreneurs, I hope, will find the book interesting and useful.

Happy reading!

(Dharmendra Pradhan)

सबको शिक्षा, अच्छी शिक्षा

MOE - Room No. 301, 'C' Wing, 3ʳᵈ Floor, Shastri Bhavan, New Delhi-110 001, Phone : 91-11-23782387, Fax : 91-11-23382365
E-mail : minister.sm@gov.in

iii

Acknowledgement

I want to express my deepest gratitude to Mr. Tanmoy Shankar Bhattacharyea, whom I have known for the past four years. He has become a fatherly figure and an inspiring mentor in this short time, profoundly shaping my recent entrepreneurial journey. His wisdom, insight, and unwavering belief in my potential have not only shaped the way I navigate challenges but have also been instrumental in helping me bring this book to life.

When I shared my idea of writing this book, Tanmoy Sir offered his full support, providing invaluable advice on organising my thoughts and structuring my experiences into a coherent narrative. He guided me through the intricate process of composition, encouraging me to reflect deeply on the lessons I've learned and to share them in a way that could benefit others. His attention to detail, patience, and constructive feedback at every stage were vital in refining the content of this book.

In addition to his mentorship in writing, Tanmoy Sir played an essential role in helping me navigate the complexities of publishing. His connections, insights into the publishing world, and tireless encouragement ensured that this book got into readers' hands. Without his unwavering guidance, this project would not have been possible. For this, I am deeply grateful.

Prologue

"Mantre Tirthe Dwije Deve Daivagye Bheshaje Gurau;
Yadrishi Bhavana Yasya Siddhir Bhavati Tadrishi"

"मन्त्रे तीर्थे द्विजे देवे दैवज्ञे भेषजे गुरौ ।
याहशी भावना यस्य सिद्धिर् भवति ताहशी ॥"

"In mantras, in sacred places, in the learned, in deities, in astrologers, in medicines, and teachers-whatever your faith, so shall be your success."

This ancient Sanskrit verse encapsulates a fundamental principle: our beliefs and intentions shape our outcomes. This book is not a self-congratulatory tale but a humble sharing of my 42-year entrepreneurial journey and insights.

My entrepreneurial journey can be summarised by the equation "$E = MC^3$." This concept, which I call the 'Theory of Relativity for Entrepreneurs', represents *Entrepreneur, Management, Capacity, Collaboration, and Capital.* These pillars have guided me throughout my career. I hope this book inspires others to become job creators and experience entrepreneurship's immense fulfilment and lasting value.

This book is a testament to the theory of relativity in entrepreneurship, structured into 12 chapters, each chronicling a significant phase of my journey. These 12 chapters have been clubbed in 4 parts to narrate how each chapter is a sequel to the previous chapter. Part 1 is named *Wandering Within, Seeking Self, demonstrating how* the Seeds of Change started working within me, prompting me to develop the first C-Capacity. I narrated my resilience in hosting these seeds of change in its sequence.

Part II of the book captioned *Unlocking the C - Capacity &
Collaboration,* spread over three chapters, delves deeper into
how my entrepreneurial capacity was developed, the lessons
learned, and my swing between Highs and Lows of Ambition,
remembering Ratan Tata's words – "If you walk alone, you can
walk fast, but if you walk together, you can walk far."

Part III of the book hovers around two chapters with the flag of
facing the Third "C" – *Capital Challenge*. I have realised the need
for collaboration as an academic foundation of entrepreneurship
and its practical application in scaling a business. Ancient
wisdom from the Bhagavad Gita and Chanakya has shaped my
understanding of business and leadership.

Part IV *Scaling Up with Collaboration* is a little long and has five
chapters. The reason is that they are genuine and have happened
around me. Suppose if I do not share it with my readers. In that
case, I shall not be able to communicate how the evolution from
a hands-on entrepreneur to a strategic manager has been possible,
achieving growth and heading for a prospective future.

One apology!

The reader may find the book is *'infested with'* quotations. It is
true. The reason is that since childhood, I have been an avid
reader of books and cannot resist collecting and remembering
these invaluable lines. These 'lines' are not delimiting me but are
the lifeline of my growth. Please excuse me one more time. If I
do not share this quotation with you, it will be a gross injustice to
the book and my thoughts. I hope you find inspiration,
motivation, and perhaps a new perspective on being an
entrepreneur while you go through the book.

"Udyamena Hi Siddhyanti Kāryāṇi Na Manorathaiḥ;
Na Hi Suptasya Siṃhasya Praviśanti Mukhe Mṛgāḥ"

"उद्यमेन हि सिद्ध्यन्ति कार्याणि न मनोरथैः ।
न हि सुप्तस्य सिंहस्य प्रविशन्ति मुखे मृगाः ॥"

"Success in tasks comes through effort, not through mere wishes.
Just as deer do not enter the mouth of a sleeping lion."- Chanakya
Niti, Chapter 2, Verse 10

Contents

Part 1

Wandering Within, Seeking Self

"Dreams are the seeds of change. Nothing ever grows without a seed, and nothing changes without a dream." - Debby Boone.

Chapter 1

The Seeds of Change

I grew up in a small village where life was simple, and dreams were as vast as the open fields that stretched beyond the horizon. My childhood was filled with the tranquillity of rural life, where the chirping of birds and the rustle of leaves in the wind marked the days. Despite the simplicity of our surroundings, my mind was always buzzing with curiosity and a hunger for knowledge. I found joy in learning, and it wasn't long before I emerged as the top student in my class.

My teachers recognized the spark in me, nurturing it with encouragement and praise. My family, too, held high hopes for my future. They saw in me the potential to break free from the confines of village life and make something of myself. From a young age, I was driven by a single, unshakable dream: to become a doctor. I was captivated by the idea of healing others and making a tangible difference in people's lives. It was a dream that seemed both noble and achievable. My path appeared clear: excel in my studies, get into medical school, and fulfil the almost preordained destiny. But as the saying goes, *"The only constant in life is change."* - Heraclitus.

A Twist of Fate

Life, however, has a way of throwing curveballs when we least expect them. After completing class 12, I was poised to take the medical entrance exams, the crucial step that would bring me closer to my dream. But just as I was about to embark on this critical journey, fate intervened in the form of a severe illness.

Jaundice struck me down, a debilitating condition that sapped my energy and confined me to bed for weeks.

The illness was more than just a physical setback; it was a blow to my spirit. I felt helpless as I laid in bed, watching my friends move forward with their plans. The future I had so carefully planned seemed to be slipping away, one painful day at a time. The physical weakness was bearable, but the mental and emotional toll was far more devastating. For the first time, I felt my dreams were out of reach.

When I finally recovered, it was too late to sit for the medical entrance exams that year. The disappointment was profound, but life offered me a new opportunity - an offer to study at the prestigious Narendrapur Ramakrishna Mission. This institution was renowned for its academic excellence, and being accepted there was an honour. However, there was a catch: while my heart was still set on becoming a doctor, I was only offered a place to study Physics as an Honors subject. With no other options available, I reluctantly accepted.

It felt like my destiny was being decided for me, and the future I envisioned was slipping further out of reach. The dream of becoming a doctor was slowly fading, replaced by a reality I hadn't planned for and didn't particularly want. It was as if the universe had redirected my path, forcing me to navigate a course I hadn't chosen.

Struggles and Hard Choices

My time at Narendrapur was brief but marked by deep internal conflict. The weight of not following my true passion left me feeling lost and disconnected from my studies. Physics was a subject I had excelled in during school, but now it felt like a burden. I couldn't find joy in the subjects that defined my future. Instead of being a stepping stone to success, my studies became a source of frustration and despair.

The atmosphere at Narendrapur, despite its academic rigour, couldn't lift my spirits. I felt like I was living someone else's life, following a path that wasn't meant for me. Every day, the sense of being trapped grew more robust, and the depression that followed made it difficult to focus on my studies. Eventually, the emotional strain became too much to bear. I made the difficult decision to leave Narendrapur and return home.

This choice to abandon a secure path in pursuit of my original dream was met with disappointment by my parents. They couldn't understand why I would give up such a promising opportunity. From their perspective, I was throwing away a stable future for a dream that seemed increasingly out of reach. Their disapproval weighed heavily on me, adding to the considerable burden of uncertainty and self-doubt.

After returning home, I was determined to try again for medical school. I threw myself into my studies with renewed vigour, hoping my efforts would pay off this time. But despite all my hard work, I failed to gain admission. This failure was devastating. It forced me to confront the harsh reality that life doesn't always go according to the plan. The dream I had held onto for so long was slipping away, and I was left to face the daunting question: What next?

A New Path in the City

Amid this uncertainty, I made a drastic decision-I ran away from home. I needed to escape the expectations, the disappointments, and the sense of failure that had begun to suffocate me. I ended up in Uttarpara, a small town not far from Kolkata, where I found refuge in a mess bari, a shared residence with minimal comforts. The other residents were commerce students, aspiring Chartered and Cost Accountants, all working toward clear goals. They were focused and driven and seemed to have their futures mapped out while I grappled with my doubts.

The mess bari was a far cry from the comforts of home. The food was scarce, the living conditions were cramped, and the future was uncertain. But despite the overwhelming uncertainty, I knew I had to survive. With the bit of money I had, I enrolled in a nearby college. But this was only the beginning of a new challenge. To stay in the city and continue my education, I needed to earn ₹50 every day-just enough to cover my food, lodging, and college fees.

This daily struggle to earn ₹50 became the defining period of my life. Every day was a battle to make ends meet. I took on small jobs-anything that would help me earn those crucial ₹50 each day. The work was hard, the hours were long, and the pay was meagre, but it was a necessary struggle.

Lessons in Resilience

As I reflect on those challenging days in Uttarpara, I am reminded of the stories of several eminent business figures who, like me, faced setbacks early in their careers but used those experiences to fuel their later successes.

Lee Iacocca, for example, was famously fired from Ford despite his many contributions, including developing the iconic Mustang. Instead of letting this setback define him, Iacocca went on to rescue Chrysler from the brink of bankruptcy, turning it into one of the most profitable car companies in America. His story is a testament to resilience and the ability to turn failure into a stepping stone for more significant achievements.

Similarly, Shiv Khera, now a renowned motivational speaker, started his career with humble beginnings, working as a car washer and a life insurance agent. Despite facing numerous challenges, Khera didn't give up. He used his experiences to build a successful career, inspiring millions with his message that success is about persistence, hard work, and self-belief.

Dhirubhai Ambani, the founder of Reliance Industries, also faced significant challenges in his early life. Starting his career as a small-time worker in Yemen, he returned to India with a vision to build something extraordinary. His journey from selling bhajias to becoming one of India's most influential industrialists is a story of grit, determination, and an uneasy belief in his dreams.

In my journey, I see parallels to these stories. My struggles were not just obstacles but opportunities to grow, learn, and redefine my path. Like Iacocca, Khera, and Ambani, I realized that the key to success lies in how you respond to setbacks. These experiences taught me the importance of resilience, adaptation, and the willingness to start over when necessary.

In the context of the Entrepreneur's Theory of Relativity (E=MC³), where M stands for Management and C for Capacity, Capital, and Collaboration, my early struggles in Uttarpara can be seen as the development of my Capacity. The challenges I faced were the crucible in which my potential was tested and expanded. Each day's survival was a lesson in resourcefulness, teaching me how to maximize my limited resources and push the boundaries of what I could achieve.

This foundation is the basis upon which I would build my career and, eventually, my business. Like Dhirubhai Ambani, who transformed his early challenges into opportunities for growth, I learned that true success is not just about having a dream but about having the capacity to make that dream a reality, no matter the obstacles.

This chapter of my life was about survival, learning, growing, and laying the groundwork for the future. The resilience I developed, the Capacity to adapt and persevere, would become the cornerstones of my entrepreneurial journey. Looking back, I see that these early struggles were not just challenges to overcome; they were the seeds of change that would eventually grow into the dreams I had yet to realize.

Citations:

1. Iacocca Lee, and William Novak. *"Iacocca": An Autobiography*. New York: Bantam Books, 1984.

2. Khera, Shiv. *"You Can Win": A Step-by-Step Tool for Top Achievers*. New Delhi: Macmillan India Ltd, 1998.

3. Ambani, Dhirubhai, and Hamish. *"The Polyester Prince": The Rise of Sydney*. McDonald: Allen & Unwin, 1998.

Chapter 2

A Journey of Resilience

"Success is not the key to happiness. Happiness is the key to success. If you love what you are doing, you will be successful."
- Albert Schweitzer

The mess bari where I lived in Uttarpara was a modest place, far removed from the comforts of home. It had one main room, a small kitchen, a veranda converted into a room, and two small rooms. Since I was a college student and needed a quiet place to study, I was allotted one of the small rooms. It was a tight space, just enough for a 6-foot by 3-foot bed and a small rack to keep my books. My other belongings were stored under the bed. It wasn't much, but it was still home for now.

Thus, living in such a confined space made it easy for me to feel overwhelmed by my challenges. But the limited space also had its benefits-it forced me to focus, block out distractions, and think creatively about how to make the best of my situation.

Meeting Fullu Bhaiya and Radha Bhabi

On the other side of the house lived a Marwari saree vendor, whom everyone in the mess bari affectionately called Fullu Bhaiya. He was a kind and pleasant man, always ready with a smile, and his wife, Radha Bhabi, was known for making the most fantastic tea. Their warmth provided comfort in a place that otherwise felt foreign and unfamiliar.

One day, as I was sipping tea in the small courtyard, I had noticed earlier that Fullu Bhaiya usually returned home by 4:30 in the afternoon. He would then unload his stock of sarees and settle in for the evening. Thus, the idea of watching him began to form in my mind. What if I could use his saree stock after he was done for the day to make some extra money?

With some hesitation, I approached Fullu Bhaiya with my idea. I asked him if he would allow me to sell his sarees door-to-door in the neighbourhood after 4:30 pm. At first, he was reluctant. He knew I was a bright student and thought I should focus on my studies rather than getting involved in something as time-consuming as selling sarees. But I shared my story with him the struggles I faced, the financial burden that weighed on me, and my desperate need to earn money to survive and stay in college.

 After thinking it over, he finally agreed. His exact words were, *"Bhai, tum padhe-likhe ho, yeh kaam tumhare liye nahi hai, par agar yeh tumhari madad kar sakta hai, toh koshish kar lo"*

("Brother, you are educated, this work is not for you, but if it can help you, then give it a try"). His words were filled with concern but also with understanding. He knew that this wasn't about ambition - it was about survival.

This situation reminded me of Howard Schultz from Starbucks. Before he became the CEO and turned Starbucks into the global coffeehouse chain it is today, Schultz had a humble beginning. He grew up in a public housing in Brooklyn, New York, where his father struggled to make ends meet. Schultz's experience with poverty and his desire to help his family led him to pursue every opportunity, no matter how small. Like Schultz, who took a small coffee shop and transformed it into a global brand, I saw a chance to sell sarees-not as an end, but as a means to something greater.

And so, my bicycle and I began a new journey as a saree seller. Every afternoon after 4:30, I would load up my bicycle with a selection of sarees from Fullu Bhaiya's stock and set off to the nearby neighbourhoods. My pitch was simple yet effective: "Sarees for sale! Factory seconds with small, unnoticeable defects! Aunties, Boudis, please take a look. It's free to browse-buy if you like something!"

At first, I was nervous. I had never done anything like this before, and I wasn't sure how people would react. But as I made my rounds, I discovered that my sincerity and the quality of the sarees spoke for themselves. The women in the neighbourhood were curious, and many were pleasantly surprised by the good deals I offered. Surprisingly, I earned a profit of ₹30 on my first day. It wasn't a huge amount, but it was enough to cover my daily expenses for food, lodging, and college fees. More importantly, it gave me a sense of hope and independence. I was no longer just surviving-I was starting to take control of my life, one saree at a time.

This small success marked the beginning of a new chapter in my life. Selling door-to-door sarees wasn't just about making money but proving that I could overcome life's challenges. Each sale, each satisfied customer, brought me a step closer to the future I was trying to build. In those moments, pedalling from door to door, I began to see the possibilities of what I could achieve.

The Transition from Saree Seller to Tutor

However, my new venture didn't go unnoticed. My landlord, a school teacher, soon found out about my side business and decided to have a conversation with me. One day, he summoned me to talk. He was a kind man, but I could tell he was concerned. He asked why I, a college student, was selling sarees instead of focusing on my studies.

I explained everything to him - how I had ended up in Uttarpara, my financial struggles, and my desperate need to earn money to support myself. His wife, a school teacher, joined the conversation as I spoke. They listened carefully and offered snacks and a new perspective instead of reprimanding me.

His wife suggested I consider giving tuition to earn money instead of selling sarees. It was a brilliant idea, but I had one primary concern: I didn't know anyone in the area who would need a tutor. Understanding my dilemma, the landlord and his wife offered to help. They knew many families in the neighbourhood and promised to find students who needed tutoring. True to their word, they soon arranged for five students who required help with their studies.

It marked the beginning of a new chapter in my life. I transitioned from being a saree seller to becoming a tutor, a role aligned more with my abilities and goals. Not only did it provide me with a steady income, but it also allowed me to focus on my studies while helping others with theirs.

This shift from selling sarees to tutoring was a crucial turning point. It was more than just a change in how I earned money - it was a step toward stability and a way to use my strengths to build a better future. My landlord's and his wife's support allowed me to focus on what truly mattered: my education and personal growth.

I began my tutoring journey with just five students, one of whom stood out. This particular student, Souvik, was from a local ICSE school and quickly became my best student. A perfect blend of innocence and intelligence, he became my beacon of hope during those early days. Under my guidance, he excelled in his studies, and his success did not go unnoticed. He spread the word about my teaching and soon brought eight more students to me. It marked the start of my first official batch, which I proudly named "Ascent Tutorial."

The growth of Ascent Tutorial mirrored the journey of Steve Jobs and Steve Wozniak in the early days of Apple. They started in a garage with a vision and a handful of resources, but through persistence and dedication, they built one of the most valuable companies in the world. Like them, I was starting small, with just a few students, but I had a vision of something much more significant. Each new student, each success story, was a step towards realizing that vision.

The Growth of Ascent Tutorial

The success of Ascent Tutorial didn't happen overnight, but it grew steadily, fueled by the dedication and hard work I put into each lesson. Among the students in that first batch was Prerna, who would later become a distinguished Chartered Accountant (CA) and Company Secretary (CS), serving as the past CFO and now the Internal Auditor in my company. Seeing my students succeed gave me immense satisfaction and fueled my passion for teaching.

In just one year, the number of students at Ascent Tutorial grew from five to thirty, and within three years, that number soared to two hundred. The modest room in the *Mess Bari* once filled with just a handful of students, now echoed with the sounds of eager learners. Ascent Tutorial wasn't just a place for learning-it became a community. I poured my heart and soul into teaching, using various digital tools and innovative methods to make learning more engaging and effective.

My approach differed from traditional teaching methods, which quickly earned me recognition as the young tutor of the town for

ICSE board students. By the time I completed my graduation at 21, I had already established a strong identity in the education sector. Ascent Tutorial became known for its commitment to excellence, and students from all over the area sought guidance.

Looking back, my journey from a saree seller to a tutor was a testament to the power of resilience and adaptability. My challenges during those early days in Uttarpara were daunting, but they shaped me into who I am today. The modest mess bari, the cramped room, the brief stint as a saree seller-all of these experiences were stepping stones that led to the creation of Ascent Tutorial.

I often think about the kindness of the people I met along the way-Fullu Bhaiya, who gave me a chance to earn my first income in Uttarpara, and my landlord and his wife, who recognized my potential and helped me find a more sustainable way to support myself. Their support was crucial in helping me navigate the difficult circumstances I found myself in.

In those moments of uncertainty, it would have been easy to give up or settle for less. However, my small successes, whether selling a saree or helping a student excel in their studies, gave me the confidence to keep pushing forward. Each step, no matter how small, was a move toward building something bigger and better.

"I have not failed. I've just found 10,000 ways that won't work."
- Thomas Edison

This chapter of my life taught me the importance of adaptability and persistence. When one path closed, another opened, and it was up to me to recognize and seize the opportunities that came my way. The transition from selling sarees to tutoring was not just a change in occupation but a shift in mindset. It was about recognizing and using my strengths to create value for myself and others.

This experience also reinforced the importance of community and collaboration. The people I met in Uttarpara were instrumental in helping me find my footing during a challenging time. Their willingness to help, belief in my potential, and encouragement were invaluable. It reminded me that success is rarely a solo journey - it's often the result of collective effort and mutual support.

As I continued to grow Ascent Tutorial, the lessons I learned during those early days stayed with me. They became the foundation upon which I built my future ventures. The journey from a small room in a mess bari to running a successful tutorial was just the beginning. It was a journey that would take me to new heights, challenges, and opportunities.

Reflecting on this chapter, I see it as a transformative journey. Adversity fueled my resilience, and perseverance became my strength. This path, though challenging, laid the foundation for my future. The lessons learned in building Ascent Tutorial would continue to shape my approach to business and life, guiding me through future successes and challenges.

Citations:

1. Schweitzer, Albert. *"Out of My Life and Thought"*: *An Autobiography*. Baltimore: Translated by C.T. Campion. Johns Hopkins University Press, 1998.

2. Schultz, Howard. *"Pour Your Heart into* It": *How Starbucks Built a Company One Cup at a Time*. New York: Hyperion, 1997.

3. Isaacson, Walter. *"Steve Jobs"*: *The Exclusive Biography*. New York: Simon & Schuster, 2011.

4. Edison, Thomas A. *"The Diary and Sundry Observations of Thomas Alva Edison"*. New York: Funk & Wagnalls, 1948.

Part 2

Unlocking the C - Capacity & Collaboration

"The capacity to learn is a gift; the ability to learn is a skill; the willingness to learn is a choice." - Brian Herbert

Chapter 3

Capacity Dances with Destiny

By the age of 22, my life had taken a significant turn. The success of Ascent Tutorial had provided me with enough income to enhance my standard of living, and in a small town like mine, I was already seen as something of a success story. After all, not many young people could claim to be financially independent, let alone successful entrepreneurs, at such an age. I took pride in my reputation as a dedicated and influential tutor. Ascent Tutorial wasn't just a business; it was a testament to the hard work and perseverance that had gotten me to that point. Yet, despite the financial stability, I grappled with an unexpected and unsettling feeling: uncertainty.

It was strange. Here I was, with more money than I had ever imagined earning at this age, yet I felt increasingly insecure about my future. It wasn't just the usual anxiety that comes with adulthood. A more profound, pervasive sense of doubt seemed to creep into my thoughts at every turn. Questions now consumed the bright student who had once been so sure of his path. What if this was it? What if my life had peaked at 22? The weight of these questions bore down on me heavily.

The Pressure of Expectations

Adding to this confusion was the pressure from my family. Government jobs were regarded as the most significant achievement in our society. They offered a steady income, a respected social status, and, most importantly, job security. Like many others, my family believed a government position was the safest and most respectable route for someone like me. They encouraged me to take this path, sometimes gently, not so gently. To them, it was the logical next step in my life.

So, to align with their expectations, I tried my hand at a few government exams. I still remember the gruelling hours of preparation, the relentless memorization of facts, and the dry, lifeless material I forced myself to absorb. The worst part was that I succeeded in several of these exams. I was offered positions that would have made my family proud. But with each success, I felt a growing disconnect. These paths didn't align with my aspirations or interests. They felt like detours rather than destinations. The thought of spending my life in a government office, performing tasks without objective meaning, filled me with dread.

I realized that I was still searching for something more - a calling that resonated with who I was at my core. I wasn't willing to live a life of unfulfillment, simply following expectations. I tried to find a path that truly spoke to me and would allow me to grow, learn, and make a meaningful impact.

The IT/ITES Sector: A New Frontier

In 2005, as I was grappling with these internal conflicts, the world around me was changing rapidly. The IT and IT-enabled services (ITES) sectors were booming. The internet was no longer a luxury; it was becoming necessary, transforming how businesses operated. With its vast pool of talented and English-speaking youth, India was at the forefront of this digital revolution. The promise of technology was all around me, and it was impossible to ignore.

I decided to explore this new frontier, feeling the need for a change. The IT/ITES sector seemed to hold the potential I sought - a dynamic, innovative, and constantly evolving field. It was a world far removed from the traditional paths I had considered. Here was a space where I could learn new skills, challenge myself, and perhaps find the sense of purpose I had been searching for.

I enrolled in a reputed hardware and networking training centre, determined to gain new skills that could open up more opportunities. The rigorous course demanded a lot from me, but I welcomed the challenge. The technical jargon, the complex diagrams, the intricate workings of networks all of it was new, and all of it was exciting. I found myself diving into the material with the same passion I had once reserved for my studies in school.

After months of intense study, I completed the course. Soon after, I was offered a job as a trainer with a salary of ₹5,000 per month. At the age of 23, this was a pivotal moment. The offer was modest compared to what I had earned from Ascent Tutorial, which gave me four times that income. Yet, I chose to accept the job. Why? Because I saw it as an opportunity to grow and expand my knowledge and skills in a fascinating field.

The Value of Experience Over Money

Looking back, it might seem strange that I would choose a job that paid much less than I had already earned. But for me, this decision wasn't about money. It was about experience. I had built a successful business as a tutor, but I knew that if I wanted to grow, I needed to step out of my comfort zone and challenge myself in new ways. This job offered me the chance to do just that.

My decision to join the training centre did not go unnoticed by the management. They soon recognized something in me that I hadn't fully realized - my sales potential. One day, the top management called me in for a meeting. They told me,

"Tu training ka banda nahi, sales ka banda hai" ("You're not a training guy, you're a sales guy"). They saw the blend of technical knowledge and commercial acumen within me and offered me a position on the sales team with a doubled salary.

While this acknowledgement was flattering, the way it was presented left me feeling uneasy. It hurt my self-esteem and conflicted with my vision of where I wanted to take my career. I hadn't come to the training centre to sell products but to learn, grow, and deepen my understanding of technology. Being pigeonholed as a "sales guy" felt like a reduction of my abilities, narrowing my potential. I'd seen this happen to others—people with immense talent stuck in roles that didn't match their abilities.

Learning from the Greats

At this moment, it reminded me of the stories of several eminent entrepreneurs who faced similar crossroads. Take Steve Jobs, for example. After being ousted from Apple, the company he co-founded, Jobs didn't let the rejection define him. Instead, he used the opportunity to explore new ventures, creating next and pixar, both of which played pivotal roles in the tech and entertainment industries. Job's story is a powerful reminder that sometimes the world sees something in us that we haven't yet discovered, but aligning this with our vision and values is crucial.

Similarly, when faced with setbacks in his early entrepreneurial days, Dhirubhai Ambani didn't allow himself to be confined by what others thought he should do. Instead, he pushed forward with his vision, ultimately building Reliance into a massive conglomerate. Ambani's journey, marked by resilience and an unshakable belief in his vision, triumphed over adversity.

Then there's Warren Buffett, one of the world's most successful investors. Buffett's early years were not marked by immediate success. He faced numerous challenges and doubts from those around him, especially when he began his investment partnership. However, Buffett stayed true to his unique investment philosophy, which focused on long-term value rather than short-term gains. His story teaches us the importance of staying true to your beliefs, even when others might not see the potential you do.

These stories reinforced a critical lesson for me: while it's important to recognize and cultivate the skills others see in you, it's equally important to stay true to your vision. Success, after all, is not just about what you achieve but about how you achieve it.

A Bold Decision

Uncomfortable with the approach and feeling that my value was being reduced to just sales potential, I made a bold decision. The very next day, I resigned from the job. It was a difficult choice with a fair share of doubt and second-guessing. Was I being too idealistic? Was I turning down an opportunity that could have led to a secure and lucrative career? These thoughts plagued me in the days that followed. But deep down, I knew that I had made the right choice. I knew that I had to stay true to myself.

As I walked away from the training centre, I couldn't help but think about Henry Ford, the pioneering founder of Ford Motor Company. Ford didn't invent the automobile, but he revolutionized the manufacturing process with the assembly line, making cars affordable for the masses. His vision wasn't just about building cars but transforming society by making transportation accessible to everyone. Ford's capacity to innovate and see the bigger picture resonated deeply with me.

Ford's story is one of resilience and innovation but also about staying true to one's vision. Ford had faced his fair share of failures and setbacks before he struck gold with the Model T. He was often criticized and even ridiculed for his ideas, but he didn't let that deter him. He had a vision and was committed to seeing it through, no matter what.

Inspired by the Business Model

Even though I left the job, something about the institute's structure and business model stayed with me. How the institute operated, the blend of technical training with business acumen, and the overall model intrigued me. It sparked a new aspiration to build something similar with a vision and approach resonating with my values.

I found myself reflecting on Narayan Murthy, the co-founder of Infosys. Murthy started with a small team and a global vision to provide quality software services. Infosys wasn't just a company; it was a dream to put India on the map as a leading provider of IT services. Murthy's journey was not just about capitalizing on the IT boom but about building a company rooted in values, integrity, and a commitment to excellence. His capacity to lead and inspire others to share in his vision was vital to Infosys's success.

Like Murthy, I realized that the path to success was about more than just financial gain. It was about building something meaningful that could have a lasting impact. I began to dream of creating an institute that combined the best aspects of technical training with a robust business model. This institute didn't just teach skills but also instilled values and a sense of purpose in its students.

This chapter marked a pivotal shift in my life, transcending a mere career change. It was a voyage of self-discovery, where I embraced my inner potential and laid the foundation for future endeavours.

Capacity, a cornerstone of my Entrepreneur's Theory of Relativity, extends beyond mere ability. It's about the potential for growth, innovation, and creation. It requires a vision that transcends the present and the courage to pursue it, even when it means leaving familiar territory.

As I embarked on this journey, I recognized and nurtured my potential. I understood that life isn't merely about sustenance but building a lasting legacy. Inspired by entrepreneurial pioneers like Ford, Ambani, Jobs, Buffett, and Murthy, I realized that success lies in today's achievements and cultivating the capacity for tomorrow's growth.

This experience marked a significant turning point in my journey. It taught me the importance of staying true to oneself, even when presented with seemingly attractive opportunities. More importantly, it inspired me to think bigger and dream of building something that could have a lasting impact.

A New Vision for the Future

As I moved forward from this experience, I began to lay the foundation for the future. The idea of creating an institute that combined the best aspects of technical training with a robust business model began to take shape in my mind. It was a vision that would take time to develop, but I knew it was achievable with the right mindset and approach.

I remembered the stories of the great entrepreneurs who had come before me, each of whom demonstrated that Capacity is not just about what you can do today but what you can build for tomorrow. I knew that if I wanted to succeed, I had to continue expanding my Capacity, learning, growing, and pushing the boundaries of what I thought was possible.

This chapter in my life was about more than finding a new career path; it was about finding myself. It was about discovering what I could and realizing that the journey to success is continuous growth, learning, and adaptation.

As I embarked on this new journey, I knew I was on the right path. I knew I could achieve my dreams, no matter how big or challenging they might seem. And I knew that this was just the beginning.

Citations:

1. Iacocca, Lee, and William Novak. *Iacocca: An Autobiography*. New York: Bantam Books, 1984.

2. Isaacson, Walter. *Steve Jobs: The Exclusive Biography*. New York: Simon & Schuster, 2011.

3. Ambani, Dhirubhai, and Hamish: *The Polyester Prince: The Rise of Sydney*. McDonald: Allen & Unwin, 1998.

4. Ford, Henry. *My Life and Work*. New York: Garden City Publishing Co., Inc., 1922.

5. Buffett, Warren, and Lawrence A. Cunningham. *The Essays of Warren Buffett: Lessons for Corporate America*. 4th ed. Hoboken: Wiley, 2015.

6. Murthy, Narayana, and Sudha Menon. *A Better India: A Better World*. New Delhi: Penguin Books India, 2009.

Chapter 4

The Lessons of Failure

"Success is not final, failure is not fatal: It is the courage to continue that count." - Winston Churchill.

By the age of 24, in 2007, I stood at another crossroads in my entrepreneurial journey. The success of Ascent Tutorial had provided me with a solid foundation, but I knew I wanted to do more. The small-scale tuition classes that had given me financial independence and local recognition was just the beginning. I felt a growing desire to expand my vision, to move beyond school-level tuition and venture into more diverse educational opportunities. It was with this mindset that I founded the Indian Institute of Manpower Development (IIMD).

IIMD represented a significant shift in my approach to education. Unlike Ascent Tutorial, which focused on school subjects, IIMD was designed to offer a more structured and diversified platform, catering to students aspiring to enter professional courses. It was my first step into a more formalized educational institution, and it was an ambitious one. I knew I couldn't do it alone to realise this vision.

Growing Pains and Gains at 24

In founding IIMD, I knew I needed expertise in areas outside of my strengths. While I was confident in my ability to teach Mathematics and guide students in analytical thinking, I realized that to succeed genuinely, I needed to bring in others who could complement my skills. I partnered with an eminent local teacher specialising in English and General Knowledge, subjects critical for students preparing for competitive exams like the

Management Aptitude Test (MAT). Together, we began offering coaching for MAT, marking the first significant expansion of my educational endeavours.

The initial success we achieved with MAT coaching was encouraging. The students responded well to our methods, and the results were promising. This early success fueled my ambition to expand further. I began to dream of turning IIMD into a comprehensive coaching centre that could prepare students for various professional entrance exams. We soon decided to offer coaching for the Joint Entrance Examination (JEE), a highly competitive exam for students aspiring to enter engineering colleges in India.

To do this, I knew I needed a team of experts. I aggregated local teachers who were specialists in Physics, Chemistry, and Biology - the core subjects for JEE preparation. On paper, everything seemed perfect. We had a strong lineup of educators, a growing base of students, and a reputation that was beginning to spread beyond our local area. I was optimistic that this new venture would be as successful as my previous efforts, if not more.

The Challenge of Diverse Minds

However, as we began to scale up, I encountered challenges I had not fully anticipated. The diverse expertise of our team, which I had initially seen as our greatest strength, soon became a source of tension. Each teacher brought their methods, philosophies, and expectations to the table, and it wasn't long before these differences began to clash. The differing goals and approaches among the teachers led to difficulty in resolving conflicts.

One particular instance stands out in my memory. We were preparing for a significant marketing campaign to attract new students for our JEE coaching program. I had envisioned a coordinated effort where each teacher would contribute their expertise to showcase our strengths as a team. However, as we sat down to plan, it became clear that everyone had ideas about the campaign's focus. The Physics teacher wanted to highlight our state-of-the-art lab facilities, while the Chemistry teacher insisted that we emphasize our unique problem-solving techniques. The Biology teacher, on the other hand, believed that our success stories should take centre stage.

As the disagreements grew, it became apparent that we were not working as a cohesive unit. While admirable, each teacher's passion and dedication pulled us in different directions. I tried to mediate, to find a middle ground that would satisfy everyone, but the underlying issue was more profound than I had initially realized. The problem wasn't just about different ideas but different visions.

Failure's Feedback

Ultimately, the JEE coaching venture did not succeed as we had hoped. Despite our best efforts, the conflicts within the team affected our ability to deliver the quality of education we had promised. The students could sense the lack of unity, and our reputation began to suffer. It was a painful realization that I needed to face: this attempt was a failure.

For many, "failure" carries a heavy stigma and a sense of finality. But I've come to see it differently. I've learned that failure is not the opposite of success but a part of it. The failed venture became one of my most valuable learning experience. It taught me that entrepreneurship is not just about having a great idea or the right skills - it's also about aligning the visions and motivations of everyone involved. Without a shared goal, even the most talented team can falter.

This experience gave me a crash course in management, far more practical and insightful than anything I could have learned from a textbook. I realized that my role as an entrepreneur was to provide direction and ensure everyone on the team was moving in the same direction. The importance of shared goals, clear communication, and team cohesion became starkly clear to me.

As I reflected on this, I found inspiration in the story of Walt Disney. Disney was not just a visionary but a master of collaboration. He understood the importance of bringing together a team that shared his vision. When Disney created the first full-length animated feature film, *Snow White and the Seven Dwarfs*, many in the industry were sceptical. The project was dubbed "Disney's Folly" by critics who believed it would fail. But Disney knew that success depended on more than just his vision; it required a team that believed in it as much as he did. He carefully selected and nurtured his team, ensuring everyone shared his dream, from the animators to the composers. The result was a groundbreaking success that laid the foundation for one of the most influential entertainment companies in the world.

Similarly, Bill Gates and Paul Allen demonstrated the power of a unified vision when they founded Microsoft. While Gates was the business mind behind the venture, Allen brought in the technical expertise. Their shared vision of a computer on every desk and in every home was the driving force behind Microsoft's success. They complemented each other's strengths and worked towards a common goal, eventually creating one of the most successful companies in the history.

These stories underscored that even the most brilliant minds could benefit from collaboration. The failures I experienced with the JEE coaching venture resulted from our inability to work together as a unified team. It was a hard lesson that would shape my future endeavours.

Finding a Kindred Spirit

However, something incredibly positive came out of this challenging experience: I met Sandip Da. Sandip was a government school teacher eager to do something different and meaningful, just like I was. He had a deep passion for teaching and a genuine desire to make a difference in students' lives. Despite my setbacks, I found in him a kindred spirit - someone who shared my vision for a better, more impactful educational experience.

Our first meeting was unassuming. We were introduced by a mutual acquaintance who knew we both had similar ambitions. I still remember the modest tea stall where we discussed our ideas. As we talked, it became clear that we were on the same wavelength. We both believed in the transformative power of education and saw the potential to do more than teach; we wanted to inspire.

Over the next few weeks, our discussions grew more focused. We began to explore the possibility of working together, pooling our resources and expertise to create something more significant than the sum of its parts. Sandip Da brought his teaching skills and experience working with students from diverse backgrounds. His insights into the challenges faced by students in government schools were invaluable.

As our collaboration took shape, I couldn't help but think of the partnership between Larry Page and Sergey Brin, the founders of

Google. Page and Brin met as PhD students at Stanford University. Despite their differing approaches and frequent disagreements, they shared a vision of organizing the world's information and making it universally accessible and helpful. Their partnership, built on mutual respect and a shared goal, created one of the world's most innovative and successful companies.

Similarly, the partnership between Steve Wozniak and Steve Jobs in the early days of Apple is another example of how complementary skills and a shared vision can lead to extraordinary success. Wozniak was the technical genius who could build a computer from scratch, while Jobs had the business acumen and vision to see the commercial potential. Together, they revolutionized the personal computer industry.

My partnership with Sandip Da wasn't on the scale of Google or Apple, but the principles were the same. We were two individuals with different strengths, united by a common goal. We knew that working together could achieve something neither of us could accomplish alone.

A New Opportunity

As Sandip Da and I began to explore new possibilities, we found support from an unexpected source. One of our students had a father who was an eminent businessman in the livestock sector. He had observed our work and recognized the potential in our ideas. One day, after a particularly successful class, he approached us with an offer that would change the course of our journey.

He saw in us the same entrepreneurial spirit that had driven him in his career. He understood the challenges we faced and the risks we were taking, and he admired our determination. But more than that, he believed in our vision. He offered to support us in starting a franchised institute and even committed to investing in our venture.

It was a significant turning point for us. It wasn't just about financial support, though it was undoubtedly substantial. His endorsement and financial backing were crucial to our success. His support boosted our confidence and propelled us forward.

This experience reminded me of the importance of mentorship and support in the entrepreneurial journey. Just as Ray Kroc, the man who transformed McDonald's from a single restaurant into a global franchise, was inspired and supported by the McDonald brothers, we too, were benefiting from the guidance and backing of someone who had already walked the path of success.

Kroc's story is particularly inspiring. When he first encountered the McDonald brothers' restaurant, he was struck by the efficiency and potential of their business model. But his vision, combined with their original concept, turned McDonald's into a household name. Kroc saw potential where others didn't, and with the McDonald brothers' support, he created a global empire.

Similarly, our mentor's support was more than just financial—it was an affirmation that we were on the right path. It was a reminder that sometimes, all it takes is for someone to believe in your vision to turn it into reality.

Coupling Growth with Marriage

Around this time, my personal life also took a significant step forward. I married Sayani, my friend turned fiancée, who had been a constant source of support and encouragement throughout my journey. Sayani was not just a partner in life but also a partner in my dreams. She understood the uncertainties of being an entrepreneur but chose to stand by me, bringing stability and strength into my life.

Our marriage marked the beginning of a new chapter, where personal and professional growth went hand in hand. Sayani's belief in me, even when I doubted myself, gave me the courage to keep moving forward. She reminded me of the importance of balance - of not just focusing on work but also nurturing the relationships that mattered.

In many ways, our marriage was similar to the partnership between Bill Gates and Melinda Gates. Melinda, who joined Microsoft as a product manager, brought her unique perspective to the company. But more importantly, she became Gates's partner in life and philanthropy. Together, they founded the Bill & Melinda Gates Foundation, one of the largest private charitable foundations in the world. Their partnership extended beyond the boardroom and into every aspect of their lives, showing how a strong personal relationship can contribute to professional success.

Sayani's presence in my life brought me a new sense of purpose. She grounded me, provided emotional support, and helped me see the bigger picture. Our life together became a source of strength that fueled my entrepreneurial ambitions.

The Entrepreneur's Odyssey

The journey I embarked on at 24 was filled with failures and successes, but each step brought valuable lessons. The failed attempt at JEE coaching taught me the importance of team alignment and management. At the same time, the collaboration with Sandip Da and the support from our business mentor opened new doors for future ventures. My marriage to Sayani added a new dimension to my life, grounding me and providing the emotional support to pursue my entrepreneurial dreams.

Reflecting on these experiences, I realized they were all part of my evolution as an entrepreneur. The challenges I faced taught me resilience, the failures gave me wisdom, and the successes gave me the confidence to keep moving forward.

"Destined to Second C" - Collaboration

This chapter of my life was about more than just the lessons of failure; it was about the power of collaboration. In the context of my Entrepreneur's Theory of Relativity (E=MC³), the second "C" stands for *Collaboration*. Collaboration is not just about working with others; it's about finding the right people, aligning visions, and working together towards a common goal. It's about understanding that success is rarely a solo journey and that the best outcomes are often the result of collective effort.

My experiences at 24 taught me that collaboration is the key to success. Whether facing setbacks or celebrating victories, I realized that the right team, mentors, and support could turn dreams into reality. As I continued my entrepreneurial journey, I was determined to foster collaboration at every step.

Citations:

1. Churchill, Winston. *The Second World War: Volume V: Closing the Ring*. Boston: Houghton Mifflin Company, 1951.

2. Thomas, Bob. *Walt Disney: An American Original*. New York: Simon & Schuster, 1976.

3. Isaacson, Walter. *Steve Jobs: The Exclusive Biography*. New York: Simon & Schuster, 2011.

4. Ambani, Dhirubhai, and Hamish: *The Polyester Prince: The Rise of* Sydney: McDonald: Allen & Unwin, 1998.

5. Gates, Bill and Melinda Gates. *The Moment of Lift: How Empowering Women Changes the World*. New York: Flatiron Books, 2019.

6. John F, Love. *McDonald's: Behind the Arches*. New York: Bantam Books, 1986.

7. Gates, Bill, and Paul Allen. *Idea Man: A Memoir by the Co-founder of Microsoft*. New York: Portfolio, 2011.

Chapter 5

The Highs and Lows of Ambition

"The greatest glory in living lies not in never falling, but in rising every time we fall." - Nelson Mandela

After the failed attempt at launching the JEE coaching centre, my mind was far from at ease. The collapse of what I had hoped would be a significant expansion of my educational enterprise weighed heavily on me. The failure wasn't just a setback but a blow to my confidence. I had entered the endeavour with high hopes, believing we could build something that would make a lasting impact with the right team and resources. But the reality was harsh - managing a diverse group of educators had proven more challenging than I had anticipated, and the vision I had held so dearly crumbled before it could fully take shape.

In the wake of this failure, I found myself restless, searching for a way to redeem myself. I was driven by the desire to create something bigger, something that would prove that the failure was not a reflection of my abilities but a learning experience. However, there was a significant hurdle in my way capital. The resources I had invested in the JEE coaching centre were gone, and if I wanted to pursue any new ventures, I needed to find a way to raise funds quickly.

From Scratch to Stocks: Launching New Venture

During this period of uncertainty, I turned my attention to the stock market. The Indian stock market was booming then, and the stories of people doubling or even tripling their investments in months were everywhere. The allure of quick gains was irresistible, especially for someone in my position, desperate to rebuild and move forward. I saw the stock market as a potential lifeline, a way to generate the capital I needed to fund my next big idea.

With this mindset, I decided to dive into the world of stocks, hoping my investment would yield quick and substantial returns. I was no stranger to risk, having already taken bold steps in my entrepreneurial journey, but the stock market was a different kind of gamble. I had some savings left, and instead of letting them sit idle, I invested them, hoping to double my capital.

However, as any seasoned investor knows, the stock market is unpredictable. While it can offer significant rewards, it can also lead to devastating losses. Unfortunately, my foray into the stock market was one of the bad decisions of that time. While still on the rise, the market was more volatile than anticipated, and the stocks I had invested in did not perform as expected. Instead of doubling my capital, I saw it diminish rapidly.

Reflecting on my past investment, I realized the harsh reality of the risks associated with speculative ventures. But it wasn't entirely in vain. This early setback in the stock market taught me valuable lessons that would shape my future decisions. It introduced me to the complexities of financial markets. It planted the seed of an idea that would eventually lead me to consider listing my company on the stock exchange to raise capital. Though painful, this experience expanded my understanding of capital markets and their role in business growth.

Despite the initial losses, I wasn't ready to give up on the potential of the stock market. Instead of retreating, I decided to deepen my involvement. I recognized that while my first attempt had failed, there was still significant potential in the stock market, particularly in the broker role. Many people, like myself, were eager to invest but lacked the knowledge and experience to navigate the market effectively. It was an opportunity indeed.

I decided to start a sub-broker enterprise, becoming an investment consultant. The idea was simple: I would use the lessons I learned from my mistakes to help others make informed investment decisions. I would act as a middleman, connecting clients to the stock market and earning a commission on the trades I facilitated. This new venture was both a way to generate income and an opportunity to rebuild my lost capital.

I launched this enterprise just a few months before my marriage. It was a hectic time balancing the demands of my growing business with the preparations for my wedding. But I was driven by the belief that this was the path forward, the way to recover from my setbacks. My mornings were dedicated to teaching; I woke up at 6 AM and taught two batches of students back-to-back until 9:30 AM. Then, after a brief break, I would dive into the stock market, working as a sub-broker from 4 PM to 10 PM. In between, I continued coaching a few exceptional students in one-on-one sessions.

These were long days, stretching to 15 or 16 hours of work, but the energy was high. I was determined to make this new venture work. The Indian stock market was still booming, and the returns improved as I gathered more clients. We profited from our investments and brokerage fees, which increased our income. The progress was satisfactory, and with each successful trade, my confidence grew.

Kota Calling: Expansion Unleashed

The satisfaction of seeing my sub-broker enterprise thrive and the steady income from my coaching sessions reignited my ambition. I began to think of new ways to expand and diversify my business. Around this time, Sandip Da and I discussed possibly taking our coaching business to the next level. We had been running Ascent Tutorial successfully, but we wanted to do more something more significant that would have a broader impact.

One idea that caught our attention was the possibility of acquiring a franchise from a renowned coaching centre in Kolkata. This coaching centre had established a solid reputation for preparing students for engineering and medical entrance exams, and partnering with them could give us the brand recognition and support we needed to scale up our operations.

In November 2007, four days after my wedding, Sandip Da and I set off for Kota to explore the franchise opportunity. While most newlyweds would have been on their honeymoon, I was on a business trip. But this was a priority for me. The potential of this partnership was too significant to ignore, and I was eager to move forward. Kota welcomed us warmly, and after several discussions, we started planning the Kolkata franchise.

An Investor's Exit: Catalysing Capacity

As we laid the groundwork for the franchise, another positive development occurred. One of our student's fathers, Anirban Da, a well-established livestock businessman, expressed interest in investing in our venture. He had been impressed by his child's progress under our guidance and saw potential in our business. He recognised the opportunity and offered to invest substantial money to help us get started.

This offer was a significant boost for us. Not only did it provide the financial support we needed, but it also gave us the validation that someone with business acumen and experience believed in our vision. Anirban Da's investment came with favourable terms, and by November 2007, he had put down a token amount to formalize his commitment. This influx of capital, combined with the appreciating value of my stock portfolio, put us in a solid position to launch the franchise.

However, as often happens in business, disaster struck just when things seemed to be falling into place. In January 2008, West Bengal was hit by a severe bird flu outbreak. The epidemic devastated the poultry industry, and Anirban Da's business was deeply affected as a livestock businessman. His investments in the poultry sector began to suffer massive losses, and he quickly found himself on the brink of bankruptcy.

With this financial crisis, Anirban Da had to withdraw his investment in our venture. He approached us with soft terms, requesting the return of his capital as he tried to salvage his own business. While I understood his situation and sympathized with him, the timing couldn't have been worse for us. We were preparing for the launch, and the sudden loss of our primary investor left us scrambling for alternatives.

This situation reminded me of Howard Schultz's challenges when he first attempted to purchase Starbucks. Schultz, who later transformed Starbucks into a global coffee powerhouse, initially struggled to raise the capital needed to buy the company. His vision was clear but seemed out of reach without financial backing. Schultz faced rejection after rejection from potential investors who couldn't see his potential. However, instead of giving up, he continued to push forward, eventually securing the necessary funds and turning Starbucks into a globally recognized brand. Schultz's determination to persevere despite financial obstacles was a lesson I would hold onto during this challenging time.

With our financial backing gone and no other investors in sight, Sandip Da and I were forced to reassess our plans. After much deliberation, we decided that the best course of action was to scale down our ambitions. Instead of launching the franchise, which required significant capital investment, we pivoted to a more modest venture a BPO (Business Process Outsourcing) training centre in Dankuni.

The idea behind the BPO training centre was to capitalize on the growing demand for trained personnel in the outsourcing industry. Unlike the franchise, which required substantial upfront investment, the BPO training centre could be launched with much lower capital. It wasn't the grand vision we had initially dreamed of, but it was a practical solution given our financial constraints.

We began working on this new project in March 2008. The plan was to start small, build a reputation, and gradually expand as we gained more clients and resources. But as we would soon discover, the challenges were far from over.

A Perfect Storm

The global financial crisis hit just as we got the BPO training centre. The subprime mortgage crisis in the United States sent shockwaves through the global economy, and the Indian stock market, which had been booming, took a nosedive. The sudden market collapse wiped out a significant portion of my investments, leaving me in a dire financial situation.

The timing couldn't have been worse. The stock market crash came just as we were trying to recover from the loss of our investor. I had hoped that the returns from my stock portfolio would help fund the new venture, but instead, I found myself facing mounting losses. In a desperate attempt to salvage my investments, I took out a loan from the bank, hoping that the market would recover and allow me to recoup my losses.

But the market continued to decline, and so did my hopes of recovery. The value of my portfolio plummeted, and I was left struggling to make the monthly payments on the loan. My earnings from the sub-broker business and the coaching classes were no longer sufficient to cover the EMIs (Equated Monthly Instalments). I soon found myself in a financial predicament.

This situation was reminiscent of the struggles faced by *Elon Musk* during the 2008 financial crisis. Musk, now celebrated as one of the most innovative entrepreneurs of our time, faced the near-collapse of both Tesla and SpaceX during that period. Tesla was bleeding cash, and SpaceX had failed its first three rocket launches, leaving both companies on the brink of bankruptcy. Musk had invested almost all of his wealth into these ventures, and when the financial crisis hit, he found himself with barely enough money to keep the companies afloat. Like Musk, I faced the terrifying prospect of losing everything I had worked for. However, just as Musk's determination and resilience eventually led to the success of Tesla and SpaceX, I knew that giving up was not an option.

The financial strain took a toll on every aspect of my life. My once-thriving business was now a shadow of its former self, and my dreams of expansion seemed more distant than ever. The stress of the situation began to affect my personal life as well. My parents, who had moved to Uttarpara two years earlier, provided a roof over my head, but the sense of security I had once felt was gone. My father was deeply unhappy with how things turned out, and his disappointment was palpable.

The relationship with my wife, Sayani, also began to suffer. Our marriage started with so much promise and was filled with tension and bitterness. Sayani had a steady job and was managing her finances, but my male ego prevented me from seeking help from her. I felt a deep sense of failure not just as a businessman, but as a husband and a son. The weight of these expectations, both external and internal, was crushing.

I tried to keep up appearances, to maintain a semblance of normalcy, but inside, I was unravelling. Each day was a battle to get through the essential tasks of running the business and fulfilling my responsibilities, but the joy and energy that had once driven me were gone. I was in survival mode, trying to stay afloat in an increasingly hopeless situation.

A Turning Point: Trusting Sandip Da

Amid this turmoil, I realized that I couldn't go on like this. The burden was too significant to bear alone, and I needed to make some difficult decisions. One evening, after another exhausting day, I sat down with Sandip Da and confided in him about my situation. I told him everything the financial losses, the strain on my relationships, and the deep sense of despair that had taken hold of me.

As I spoke, I could see the concern in his eyes. He listened patiently, offering words of comfort and understanding. But when I finally told him I was considering closing the business, I could see the shock register on his face. It was a moment I had been dreading, but I knew it was necessary.

Sandip Da didn't try to dissuade me right away. Instead, he asked me to take some time to think it over and consider all the possibilities before making such a final decision. He reminded me of the successes we had achieved together and our progress despite the setbacks. He spoke of the students we had helped, the lives we had touched, and the potential that still existed.

His words gave me pause. For the first time in weeks, I allowed myself to reflect on the journey we had been on. Yes, we had faced failure and disappointment, but we had also accomplished much. The challenges we encountered were part of the process, part of every entrepreneur's learning curve.

This moment of reflection reminded me of *J.K. Rowling*, the author of the Harry Potter series. Before she became one of the best-selling authors of all time, Rowling faced numerous rejections and hardships. She was a single mother living on welfare when she conceived the Harry Potter idea. Her manuscript was rejected by multiple publishers before finally being accepted. Rowling's story is about perseverance and believing that success is possible even in the darkest times. Her determination to keep going was a powerful example of resilience, even when the odds were against her.

As I reflected, I realized that perhaps I had been too quick to see only the failures. I had been so focused on what had gone wrong that I had lost sight of what we had done right. The road had been difficult, but it wasn't without its victories. And in those victories, there were lessons - lessons that could guide us as we moved forward.

Resilience Redefined: A Shift in Perspective

In the following days, I began to regain a sense of perspective. The challenges we faced were real, but they were not insurmountable. The financial losses were significant, but they were not the end of the road. With the support of Sandip Da and the encouragement of those around me, I started to see a way forward.

I began to understand that resilience is not just about enduring hardship; it's about finding the strength to rise again after you've been knocked down. It's about learning from failure and using those lessons to build something more substantial. Closing down the business no longer seemed like the only option. Instead, I started to think about how we could rebuild—take the lessons we had learned and apply them to a new venture.

This understanding of resilience reminded me of *Thomas Edison*, one of history's greatest inventors. Edison's timeless words, 'I have not failed. I've just found 10,000 ways that won't work,' serve as a potent reminder that setbacks are merely stepping stones on the path to success. Edison faced countless failures in his quest to develop the electric light bulb, but he never gave up. Instead, he viewed each failure as a step closer to success. Despite repeated setbacks, Edison's relentless pursuit of his vision was a powerful reminder that resilience is critical to achieving great things.

Citations

1. Mandela, Nelson. *Long Walk to Freedom: The Autobiography of Nelson Mandela*. Boston: Little, Brown, 1994.

2. Schultz, Howard. *Pour Your Heart into It: How Starbucks Built a Company One Cup at a Time*. New York: Hyperion, 1997.

3. Isaacson, Walter. *Elon Musk: Tesla, SpaceX, and the Quest for a Fantastic Future*. New York: HarperCollins, 2015.

4. Rowling, J.K. *Very Good Lives: The Fringe Benefits of Failure and the Importance of Imagination*. New York: Little, Brown, 2015.

5. Edison, Thomas A. *The Diary and Sundry: Observations of Thomas Alva Edison*. New York: Funk & Wagnalls, 1948.

Part 3

Facing the Third C - The Capital Challenge

"The only way to do great work is to love what you do. If you haven't found it yet, keep looking. Don't settle." - Steve Jobs

Chapter 6

The Power of Collaboration

As I look back on the journey that brought me to this point, it's clear that entrepreneurship is a path filled with twists, turns, and unexpected challenges. My experience has taught me that success isn't a straight line-it's a winding road that requires resilience, adaptability, and a willingness to face adversity head-on. The lessons from my early days in Uttarpara prepared me for the next phase of my journey, which would test my ability to collaborate, secure capital, and build a sustainable business amidst a storm of uncertainty.

My financial situation was precarious after the setbacks with the stock market crash and the withdrawal of Anirban Da. The hope of launching a successful franchise seemed slipping through my fingers. Sandip Da and I signed a franchise agreement with a Marwari-driven organization, running a BPO training centre during this period. It was a critical move, but the financial strain left me with zero capital. The weight of the situation pressed heavily on me, and it was clear that without immediate intervention, our plans would collapse before they even began.

An Unexpected Lifeline

In times of crisis, support often comes from the most unexpected places. My wife, Sayani, had been silently observing the stress and frustration that I was going through. Despite her feelings of helplessness, she was determined to find a solution. After discussing our situation with her mother, my mother-in-law suggested a possible way out - a private lender who would provide a loan at 2% interest per month, with her guarantee.

At first, I was hesitant. Borrowing money from a private lender with such high interest rates was daunting. But as I considered the alternatives - or the lack of them - I realized this was the only option available. The terms were steep, but they gave me the needed breathing room. With the loan secured, I had three years to repay it, and I knew I had to take this chance. It was a risky move, but I felt it necessary to keep our dream alive.

With the funds in hand, I returned to work with renewed commitment. However, it wasn't long before new challenges emerged. The budget provided by the franchisor for setting up the BPO training centre soon proved wildly inaccurate. In reality, the costs were more than double what had been estimated, and the financial resources I had painstakingly secured were rapidly dwindling. It was like trying to fill a leaking bucket; no matter how much effort I put in, the resources kept slipping away. Once again, I stared into the abyss, unsure of how to move forward.

Partnering for Survival

As the financial strain deepened, I realised I couldn't navigate this storm alone. Sandip Da, ever the pragmatist, proposed a solution that, while far from ideal, could potentially save us. He suggested bringing in a new partner - a Marwari businessman known for his sharp business acumen. However, this businessman was clear about his conditions: he would invest only a limited amount and expected periodic returns.

Though a bailout in many ways, this offer was fraught with challenges. Accepting the terms meant committing to deliver returns, even when the business was in its infancy and cash flow was uncertain. But we had no other choice. The franchisor, aware of our financial troubles, began to apply immense pressure to get the centre up and running. Failure to meet the demands would result in the termination of the agreement, a scenario that would leave us worse off than before.

We agreed to the businessman's terms with no other options and brought him on board. This partnership was a delicate balancing act. While the new capital provided temporary relief, it also placed us under increased scrutiny and heightened expectations. I was constantly aware that any misstep could jeopardize the entire venture.

The situation reminded me of my early days in Uttarpara when I was forced to sell sarees door-to-door to make ends meet. Back then, the stakes were high, and the margin for error was slim. I had to adapt quickly, learn on the fly, and find creative solutions to problems I had never faced before. Those experiences taught me the importance of perseverance and pushing forward despite the odds stacked against me. Now, those same lessons were coming into play as I navigated the complexities of this new partnership.

The pressure was relentless. My financial condition was deteriorating rapidly. Every rupee I earned went towards repaying loans, leaving little for anything else. My savings depleted, my LIC premiums went unpaid, and my health insurance lapsed. The stress of the situation began to take a toll on my health. I started to gain weight, a physical manifestation of the anxiety and the long hours. My body and mind were losing shape, and my courage and positivity were tested daily.

Despite the mounting difficulties, I knew I couldn't afford to give up. I remembered the days in Uttarpara, where the struggle to survive had shaped my resilience. Back then, selling sarees door-to-door taught me the value of persistence and taking bold risks in adversity. Those lessons were more relevant now than ever.

In a surprising turn of events, another lifeline came from my father-in-law, whom Sandip Da had known from the past when Sayani was his student. Understanding our dire situation, my father-in-law offered to become our fourth partner in our venture. His involvement provided much-needed financial support and stability, bringing the team renewed hope. We named our firm *Achievers*, and with cautious optimism, we launched the BPO training centre in Dankuni.

Our local Member of Parliament inaugurated the centre, whose words of encouragement provided a much-needed morale boost. A regional manager from the franchisor's side was also present, and we developed a rapport over time. Being of the same age and sharing similar experiences, we found common ground, which helped ease some of the tensions that had been building up.

With Achievers now operational, my daily routine became more rigorous. My mornings were spent at Ascent Tutorial from 6:30 AM to 10:00 AM, followed by managing Achievers from 10:30 AM to 5:00 PM. The evenings were again dedicated to Ascent Tutorial, where I taught from 5:30 PM to 10:00 PM. It was a gruelling schedule, but amidst the chaos, I saw a glimmer of hope. The blurred vision of my future that had plagued me for so long was starting to clear, and I could feel a renewed sense of purpose guiding me forward.

Building Capacity Amidst Uncertainty

As the business stabilised, I reflected on the journey that had brought me to this point. The relentless pursuit of success amidst the challenges of new partnerships and limited resources pushed me to the brink. Still, they had also built within me a new capacity-to manage diverse minds, to navigate complex financial situations, and to lead under extreme pressure.

In those early days at Ascent Tutorial, I learned the importance of understanding the needs and motivations of different students. Each student came with their strengths, weaknesses, and goals. As a tutor, I had to adapt my teaching methods to meet these diverse needs, ensuring that each student could achieve their full potential. As an entrepreneur, I have found that the same principles apply on a much larger scale. Managing a team of diverse individuals, each with their interests and expectations, required patience, empathy, and a deep understanding of human nature.

Building Achievers wasn't just about launching a new business; it was about learning to handle the complexities of collaboration and capital. It was about understanding that success doesn't come from having all the answers but from being able to adapt, learn, and grow in the face of challenges.

This experience also reinforced the importance of trust and communication in any partnership. With Sandip Da, the Marwari businessman, my father-in-law, and the franchisor, I had to constantly manage expectations, navigate conflicting interests, and ensure that everyone remained committed to the shared goal of making Achievers a success. It wasn't easy, and there were many moments when I feared the entire venture would collapse. But by staying focused on the long-term vision and by drawing on the lessons of resilience from my past, I was able to keep the team moving forward.

As I navigated these challenges, I developed a deeper understanding of what it meant to build capacity—not just in terms of financial resources but leadership, decision-making, and personal growth. I realized that the capacity to handle difficult situations, make tough decisions, and lead others through uncertainty was just as important as the financial capital needed to run a business.

In many ways, this journey was about building a new capacity beyond the traditional measures of success. It was about developing the inner strength, resilience, and adaptability needed to face whatever challenges came our way. It was about learning to lead with empathy, build trust with others, and create an environment where everyone could contribute to the venture's success.

A New Beginning

Looking back, the journey of launching Achievers was a crucible that forged my abilities as an entrepreneur. The financial struggles, the sleepless nights, and the constant pressure were tests of my capacity to lead and innovate under duress. But they were also opportunities to build something that could last and stand the test of time.

Achievers was more than just a business venture; it was a testament to the power of collaboration and the importance of building capacity. It was a reminder that no matter the journey's difficulty, there is always a way forward if you are willing to keep pushing, believing, and building.

As we moved into the next phase of our journey, I knew the challenges were far from over. But I also knew we had laid a strong foundation built on trust, perseverance, and the willingness to take risks. This foundation would carry us through the trials ahead and serve as the bedrock for the success we were beginning to glimpse on the horizon.

In the following chapters, I will explore how these experiences continued to shape my journey and how the lessons learned during the launch of Achievers prepared me for the new challenges that awaited me. The road ahead was uncertain, but it was also full of promise, and I was ready to face it with renewed strength and determination.

Sitting in my shared cabin at the newly launched Achievers Centre, I couldn't help but reflect on how far we had come. Just a few months ago, the future had seemed bleak, filled with uncertainty and doubt. But now, there was a sense of hope, a belief that we were on the right path. The inauguration of the centre by our local Member of Parliament had been a moment of pride, a public recognition of the hard work and perseverance that had brought us to this point.

The presence of the regional manager from the franchisor's side was also a positive sign. Over time, we developed a rapport, finding common ground in our shared experiences. This relationship proved invaluable as we navigated the early days of the business. The franchisor had been demanding, placing immense pressure on us to get the centre up and running. But now, with the regional manager as an ally, I felt more confident in our ability to meet these expectations.

The launch of Achievers marked the beginning of a new phase in my life, filled with challenges and opportunities. The gruelling schedule I had taken on - balancing my work at Ascent Tutorial with my responsibilities at Achievers - was physically and mentally exhausting. But it was also gratifying. For the first time in a long while, I felt a sense of purpose and clarity about the direction I wanted my life to take.

The support of my family further strengthened this renewed sense of purpose. Sayani, a constant source of strength throughout this journey, stood by me, providing the emotional support I needed to keep going. My father-in-law's decision to become a partner in Achievers provided the financial backing we needed and brought a sense of stability to the venture. His experience and guidance made me more equipped to handle the challenges ahead.

Achievers' future was uncertain, but our momentum was undeniable. I knew we still had a long way to go, but I also knew we had the foundation to build something remarkable. The lessons of resilience, collaboration, and capacity-building I had learned along the way would continue to guide me as we moved forward.

As I looked to the future, I was filled with a sense of optimism. The road ahead would not be easy, but I was ready to face it with renewed strength and determination. Launching Achievers taught me that success is not just about financial gain it's about the relationships we build, the challenges we overcome, and the impact we have on the lives of others.

The experiences I had gone through shaped me into a more decisive, more resilient leader. Our challenges tested our limits and brought out the best in us. We had learned to work together as a team, to trust each other, and to support one another in times of need. These were the qualities that would carry us through the challenges that lay ahead and ensure that Achievers would not just survive but thrive.

As I sat in my cabin, reflecting on the journey so far, I knew that the story of Achievers was beginning. Our challenges had been complex, but they had also been transformative. They taught me that success is about reaching a destination and the journey. It's about the lessons we learn, the people we meet, and our impact on the world.

The future was uncertain, but I was ready to face it head-on. With my family's support, our team's strength, and lessons learned, I knew we had what it takes to build something remarkable. Achievers was not just a business it was a testament to the power of resilience, collaboration, and the belief that anything is possible with hard work and determination.

As we moved forward, I knew that the journey would continue to be filled with challenges, but I also knew we could overcome them. Our foundation was strong, and we would continue to grow, learn, and build something that would last with each new challenge. The story of Achievers was beginning, and I was excited to see where the journey would take us next.

Citations

1. Isaacson, Walter. *Steve Jobs: The Exclusive Biography*. New York: Simon & Schuster, 2011.

2. Schultz, Howard. *Pour Your Heart into It: How Starbucks Built a Company One Cup at a Time*. New York: Hyperion, 1997.

3. Isaacson, Walter. *Steve Jobs: The Exclusive Biography*. New York: Simon & Schuster, 2011.

4. Edison, Thomas A. *The Diary and Sundry Observations of Thomas Alva Edison*. New York: Funk & Wagnalls, 1948.

Chapter 7

Self-Mastery: Successful Collaboration

"Uddhared Atmanatmanam Na Atmanamavasadayet;
Atmaiva Hyatmano Bandhuratmaiva Ripuratmanah"

"उद्धरेदात्मनात्मानं नात्मानमवसादयेत् ।
आत्मैव ह्यात्मनो बन्धुरात्मैव रिपुरात्मनः ॥"

"Let a man lift himself by his self alone, and let him not lower himself; for this self alone is the friend of oneself, and this self is the enemy of oneself." - Bhagavad Gita, Chapter 6, Verse 5

Reflecting on my journey so far, I see that each challenge was like a stepping stone, guiding me closer to understanding the true essence of entrepreneurship. It wasn't just about overcoming barriers but finding joy in the struggle, learning from every setback, and growing stronger with each success. However, this phase of my journey - managing a professional institute - brought new challenges and lessons, particularly in collaboration and building capacity.

When we opened our training centre, my partners and I were optimistic. We believed that simply setting up the centre, hiring good trainers, and running newspaper advertisements would be enough to attract students. I thought that by distributing pamphlets and placing ads, we would soon have a flood of students eager to join our courses. But as the days passed, I realized my expectations were far from reality.

The Reality Check

The initial enthusiasm began to fade as we struggled to fill our classrooms. The numbers we had hoped for didn't materialize, and it became clear that something was missing. I had been under the illusion that opening the doors was enough, but I quickly learned that success required much more than just a physical presence.

In moments of doubt, I often remembered a phrase from childhood: *"The cow does not give milk; you have to do the milking."* This simple yet profound saying reminded me that success requires effort, strategy, and a proactive approach. You can't just wait for things to happen; you must make them happen.

With this in mind, I decided to take a more hands-on approach. We began organizing local area sensitization and mobilization camps, where we conducted seminars to counsel and motivate potential students. These seminars were not just about marketing - they were about understanding the needs of our community, addressing their concerns, and showing them how our courses could help them achieve their goals.

Taking on the role of leading these seminars was a new experience for me. Initially, speaking to large groups was intimidating, but as I began to engage with the audience, I discovered a new skill within myself. I learned how to connect with people, inspire them, and turn that inspiration into action.

Through these seminars, I understood that many of our students, especially those from rural areas, were well-educated but lacked the skills and confidence to succeed in the job market. Their biggest challenge was communication, particularly in English, a significant barrier to their confidence and employability.

Tech Skills weds Communication

Computer training was becoming increasingly popular then, but our approach was different. We offered a combination of basic computer operational skills and English communication training skills that were essential for entering the booming BPO sector. This blend of technical and soft skills became our unique selling point, setting us apart from other training centres.

These seminars weren't just about imparting knowledge and building capacity - both in myself and my students. The first "C" of my Entrepreneur's Theory of Relativity, Capacity, was now passed on to those I taught. I was helping them develop the skills they needed to be job-ready, not just in terms of technical knowledge but confidence and communication.

As I focused on helping my students build their capacity, I couldn't help but recall the teachings of Chanakya, the ancient Indian strategist and philosopher. Chanakya emphasized the importance of foresight, planning, and adaptability - qualities that I realized were essential for both my students and myself.

"Sampatti: Sukhritaih Purvair Prarthate Manasapi Yah;
Adrishyam Labhate Lakshmih Bhagyam Tasya Pradayate"

"संपत्ति: सुकृतै: पूर्वै: प्रार्थ्यते मनसापि य: ।
अदृष्टं लभते लक्ष्मी: भाग्यं तस्य प्रदायते ॥"

"The wealth and success that one desires are attained through past good deeds and hard work; fate provides fortune to those who make efforts." - Chanakya Sutra

This mindset helped me see that running a thriving training centre wasn't just about following a set formula - it required constant innovation, learning, and the ability to pivot when things didn't go as planned.

"Job Guarantee" vs. "Job Ready"

During this time, the term "Skill Development" was still relatively new in India. There was no standardization of what it meant to be skilled, and the responsibility of defining and delivering these skills fell largely on training institutions like ours. The industry was driven by the promise of "Job Guarantee," a term I had serious reservations about. I knew no institution could guarantee a job, as employment depended on many factors beyond our control.

Instead, I introduced the "Job Ready" concept to the market. Our courses were designed not to guarantee employment but to prepare students for the job market. This subtle shift in messaging allowed us to stand out in a crowded and competitive market. It was also in line with the teachings of the Bhagavad Gita, which emphasize focusing on one's duties without being overly attached to the results.

"Karmanye Vadhikaraste Ma Phaleshu Kadachana;"

"कर्मण्येवाधिकारस्ते मा फलेषु कदाचन।"

"You have the right to work but never to the fruits of your labour." - Bhagavad Gita, Chapter 2, Verse 47

To reach the potential students, I employed a strategy that was innovative but also had its challenges. I began collecting details of candidates registered with the Employment Exchange a government initiative to register job seekers and sent postcards to their addresses. This approach was a direct way to reach out to those seeking employment.

However, this strategy sometimes led to confusion. One day, a candidate came to our centre with a postcard and asked, "Where is my posting? I received a letter saying I got a job." It was a moment of realization for me, highlighting the gaps in awareness among our educated workforce. Our work was not just about skill development - it was about educating and empowering our students to navigate the complexities of the job market.

The Pressure of Expectations

As our training centre gained traction, my partners' expectations grew. I was the youngest partner by at least ten years, and the pressure to perform weighed heavily on me. Everyone looked to me for updates, decisions, and leadership. The venture's success rested on my shoulders, and I knew any failure would reflect directly on me.

But instead of being overwhelmed by this pressure, I found that it fueled my determination to succeed. The teachings of the Gita came to mind again, particularly the concept of *karma yoga* - the path of selfless action. I focused on the work, putting my energy into building the best training programs, supporting our students, and ensuring that every decision I made aligned with our long - term goals.

"Yogah Karmasu Kaushalam;"

"योगः कर्मसु कौशलम् ।"

"Yoga is excellence in action." - Bhagavad Gita, Chapter 2, Verse 50

This verse reminded me to focus on my duty without being overly concerned about the results. It was not about immediate success but building something sustainable and meaningful.

However, the financial pressures were never far from my mind. Our earnings were modest, and every rupee seemed to be allocated to repaying loans, paying trainers, or covering operational costs. The state government of West Bengal's announcement of a subsidy for students undergoing training from reputed institutes brought a glimmer of hope. This subsidy, which was to be transferred to the franchisor's account after royalty deductions, was a welcome relief. However, it also introduced a new layer of complexity to our operations.

The subsidy applied only to candidates enrolled in the Employment Exchange, and its release was to be periodic. This arrangement created a new point of contention between us and the franchisor, as the realization of these payments was fraught with delays and disagreements. Yet, I began to see these challenges not as obstacles but as opportunities to grow and strengthen our operations. Every pain point and moment of conflict was an opportunity to learn, innovate, and improve our systems.

The Wisdom of Collaboration

Through this journey, I realized that collaboration, the second "C" in my Entrepreneur's Theory of Relativity, was not just about working together but building relationships based on trust, mutual respect, and shared goals. My collaboration with my partners, my franchisor, and my students enabled us to navigate our challenges and move forward despite the difficulties.

The teachings of the Bhagavad Gita and Chanakya's strategies were philosophical concepts and practical tools that helped me stay grounded, focused, and resilient. They taught me that every challenge is an opportunity for growth, that authentic leadership is about serving others, and that success comes not from seeking results but from dedicating oneself to the work.

As I continued building our training centre, I found these ancient teachings more relevant than ever. They provided a framework for understanding the complexities of the business world, navigating conflicts, and making decisions that were profitable and aligned with our values.

Looking back on this phase of my journey, I see it as a time of intense learning and growth. It was a period that tested my limits, challenged my assumptions, and forced me to develop new capacities - both as a leader and an individual. The lessons I learned during this time would continue to shape my approach to business and life in the years to come.

As we moved forward, I knew the challenges were far from over. But I also knew I had the tools, the knowledge, and the support needed to face whatever came next. Our foundation was strong, and we would continue to grow, learn, and build something that would last with each new challenge.

The story of Achievers was beginning, and I was excited to see where the journey would take us next. With the wisdom of ancient teachings to guide me and the support of my collaborators to sustain me, I was ready to face the future with confidence and determination.

Citations:

1. Eknath, Easwaran. *Bhagavad Gita: The Bhagavad Gita: A New Translation.* Tomales, CA: Nilgiri Press, 2007.

2. Kautilya. *Chanakya: Arthashastra.* Translated by R. Shamasastry. Bangalore: Government Press, 1915.

3. Isaacson, Walter. *Steve Jobs: The Exclusive Biography.* New York: Simon & Schuster, 2011.

Part 4

Scaling Up with Collaboration

"Coming together is a beginning; keeping together is progress; working together is a success." — Henry Ford[1].

Chapter 8

Synergy for Success

A Chance Encounter and a Lasting Friendship

It was December 2010, and the chill in the air mirrored the anticipation I felt as I attended a seminar. The event was a convergence of ideas, a space where entrepreneurs like myself gathered to absorb new strategies, network with peers, and fuel the relentless drive to succeed. Little did I know that this day would introduce me to someone who would become a pivotal figure in my journey - a man whose impact would extend far beyond professional collaboration and into deep, lifelong friendship.

His name was Debjit, and he was my franchisor's newly appointed Regional Manager. He was brought in to revitalize our struggling regional business. Our unexpected meeting sparked a friendship that became a cornerstone of my career. At first glance, Debjit did not stand out. He wasn't someone whose appearance commanded attention; instead, his presence, sharp intellect, and ability to communicate clearly and confidently drew people in.

Debjit spoke with a conviction that was both inspiring and contagious. Listening to him discuss the business, the passion and understanding in him overwhelmed me. He was more than just an expert; he was an inspiring leader who could motivate others to reach their full potential.

Our connection was immediate and robust. We bonded over shared goals, a mutual understanding of the challenges ahead, and a shared vision for the future. Our camaraderie snowballed, and even our franchisor took notice. "You're on my payroll,

Debjit, but it seems like you're a team member of Abhijit Da," he remarked jokingly. Debjit, with his characteristic broad smile, acknowledged the comment without denying its truth. It was the beginning of a partnership to help us navigate the highs and lows of scaling the business to new heights.

Conflict and Collective Action

Debjit became more than just a colleague; he was a mentor and a friend. He guided me through the complexities of the business, teaching me how to spot opportunities where others saw obstacles, turn those opportunities into tangible success, and navigate the intricate dynamics of the industry. His mentorship was invaluable, but our synergy - how we complemented each other - drove our achievements. I took what I learned from him, infused it with my insights, and together, we transformed a small franchise centre into one of the top-performing centres in the country.

During this time, the business was not without its challenges. The conflict with our franchisor over the recovery of government subsidies was reaching a critical point. It was a complex issue that affected many franchisees, not just me. Recognizing the power of collective action, I began to form alliances with other franchisees. It led to the creation of "The All India Education Franchisee Welfare Association," where I served as the first General Secretary. The association quickly gained momentum, with franchisees from various educational companies joining forces. It became a platform where we could share grievances, strategize together, and confront the big players in the industry.

We were no longer isolated voices but a unified force demanding fair treatment and transparency from our franchisors. The sense of solidarity among the franchisees was empowering. We were no longer at the mercy of the franchisors; we had taken control of our narrative and destiny with that. This phase of my life was transformative. It wasn't just about growing a business; it was about understanding the power of collaboration and the collective strength of unity. The recognition I gained from my peers and the franchisor community was affirming, but the insights I gathered during this time were invaluable.

I learned about marketing and business strategies and why businesses fail and succeed. These lessons would later prove crucial as I expanded my ventures.

Finding Destiny in A French Colony

During this time, Debjit brought an opportunity to my attention that would change the course of my business. A company-owned centre in Chandan Nagar had been struggling for some time, posting consecutive losses. The franchisor was considering selling it off or shutting it down altogether. Debjit, with his sharp intuition, believed the centre had great potential. He saw that its decline was due to poor leadership, not a lack of market opportunity. He encouraged me to take over the centre, confident that under my leadership, it could thrive.

Around the same time, my personal life was undergoing significant changes. My father-in-law had passed away suddenly, and my wife was pregnant with our first child. Balancing the demands of my personal and professional life was a challenge, and the thought of taking on another centre seemed daunting. My wife, understandably anxious about our future, urged me to focus on our existing centre rather than expanding. But something inside me knew that this was an opportunity I couldn't pass up.

Capital was tight, and I faced a difficult decision. Ultimately, I chose to mortgage my wife's jewellery - without her consent - to secure the funds needed to take over the Chandan Nagar centre. It was a risky and aggressive move that could have had severe consequences for my business and marriage. However, I believed in the centre's potential and knew it could be turned around with exemplary leadership.

Debjit's unwavering support during this period cannot be overstated. He stood by me, offering advice and the emotional support I needed to navigate my personal and professional challenges. He once said, "In business, as in life, risks are not to be avoided. We should embrace them with a calculated mind and a courageous heart." His words resonated with me, giving me the strength to push forward despite the uncertainties.

The risk paid off. Under my management, the Chandan Nagar centre flourished, increasing its sales by fifteen times within a short period. It became one of the top-performing centres in the country and was recognized multiple times for its outstanding performance. This success didn't go unnoticed. Other franchisees began approaching me, offering their centres for me to manage under fixed terms. It led to a rapid expansion, and within a short span, I went from managing one centre to overseeing five.

Strategic Decision for Expansion

Each new centre presented challenges, but I was now well-equipped to handle them. The lessons from Debjit and my growing experience allowed me to approach these new ventures confidently and clearly. I began to see patterns in the business, understanding what worked and what didn't, and I used this knowledge to drive each centre to success.

My role as a franchisee underwent a significant transformation during this time. I became a key player for the company, someone they could rely on to turn around struggling centres and drive growth. But even as I expanded my operations, something else was brewing in the back of my mind. The more success I achieved, the more I contemplated possibly starting my own company to create my brand. The idea was no longer just a dream; it was becoming a plan.

By 2012, I was 29 years old and ready to take the next step in my entrepreneurial journey. The law of attraction was at work, and I could feel the pieces falling into place. The experiences I had gained, the lessons I had learned, and the relationships I had built all pointed me in one direction: toward independence, toward creating something entirely my own.

Looking back, I realize this phase of my life was about more than just scaling a business. It was about building the capacity to manage multiple ventures, understanding the true power of collaboration, and using innovative approaches to overcome financial constraints. It was also about recognizing leadership's value - guiding a business and inspiring others to see the potential within themselves.

The Path to Independence: Vision and Ambition

The journey from managing a single franchise centre to overseeing multiple successful operations was a testament to the power of collaboration and the importance of strategic decision - making. It was a period of intense personal and professional growth, and it laid the foundation for the next phase of my entrepreneurial journey - one where I would step out from the shadow of a franchisor and create a brand that was entirely my own.

As I prepared for this new chapter, I knew the lessons learned during this time would be invaluable. The partnerships I had formed, the risks I had taken, and the successes I had achieved were all part of a larger story - a story of resilience, innovation, and the relentless pursuit of a vision. As I looked ahead, I was filled with excitement and anticipation, ready to embrace whatever challenges and opportunities future would bring.

Reflecting on this journey, I recall a quote by Henry Ford: "Coming together is a beginning, staying together is progress, and working together is success."[1] This encapsulates the essence of what Debjit and I achieved together. It wasn't just about our efforts; it was about the synergy we created, how we complemented each other's strengths, and how our collaboration fueled the success of our ventures.

The story of this chapter is not just mine; it is the story of every entrepreneur who has ever faced the challenges of growth and expansion. It is the story of every leader who has ever had to make difficult decisions in the face of uncertainty. It is the story of every person who has ever dared.

Dreams & Reality: Deconstructing Success

While scaling the business, I learned the critical importance of understanding one's limits and then pushing beyond them with the proper support. I realized collaboration was not just about sharing responsibilities; it was about building a network of trust where each partner contributes uniquely to the common goal. This network allowed me to stretch my capabilities, take risks that would have been daunting alone, and achieve outcomes that far exceeded my expectations.

Looking Ahead: Lessons and Legacy

Expanding to five centres brought success and deepened our understanding of market dynamics. I began to appreciate the intricacies of local markets, the importance of adapting strategies to suit different regions, and the need for constant innovation. Each centre was like a new puzzle, and solving it required a blend of analytical thinking, creativity, and practical wisdom.

Debjit often reminded me of a fundamental principle in business: "The more you give, the more you receive." This principle guided our approach to managing the centres. We focused not just on extracting profits but on investing in our people, our processes, and our communities. We built relationships based on mutual respect and trust, creating a loyal customer base and a motivated team. This philosophy of giving back became a cornerstone of our business strategy and was instrumental in our sustained growth.

As the centres thrived, I also had to confront the challenges of managing a growing team. Leadership took on new dimensions as I transitioned from a hands-on manager to a strategic leader. I had to learn to delegate effectively, trust my team members, and empower them to take ownership of their roles. This shift was not easy, but it was necessary for the continued growth of the business.

One of the most profound lessons I learned during this time was the importance of resilience. There were moments when things didn't go as planned when setbacks threatened to derail our progress. But each time, I found strength in our collaborative network. Debjit, in particular, was a constant source of encouragement, reminding me that every challenge was an opportunity to learn and grow.

The more success we achieved, the more I began to think about the future. The idea of starting my own company and creating something entirely my own started to take shape. I began to see the potential for building a brand that reflected my values, vision, and business approach. The thought was both exhilarating and daunting, but I knew it was possible with the foundation we had built.

By 2012, I was 29 years old and ready to leap into entrepreneurship. The law of attraction, which had guided me this far, seemed to work in my favour. Opportunities began to present themselves, and I could feel the momentum building. The experiences I had gained, the lessons I had learned, and the relationships I had built all pointed me in one direction: toward independence, toward creating something uniquely mine.

As I prepared for this new chapter, I knew the road ahead would be challenging, but I was ready. The lessons learned during this time equipped me with the tools I needed to navigate the uncertainties of entrepreneurship. The partnerships I had formed, the risks I had taken, and the successes I had achieved were all part of a larger story - a story of resilience, innovation, and the relentless pursuit of a vision.

Looking back on this journey, I am reminded of the words of Steve Jobs, who once said, "Your work is going to fill a large part of your life, and the only way to be truly satisfied is to do what you believe is great work. And the only way to do great work is to love what you do."[2] These words ring valid, not just for me, but for anyone who has ever embarked on the journey of entrepreneurship.

In the end, this chapter is about more than just building a business; it is about creating a life one that is filled with purpose, passion, and the relentless pursuit of excellence. It is about understanding that success is not just about achieving your goals but about becoming the person you were meant to be.

As I continue on this journey, I know that the lessons learned during this time will continue to guide me, shaping my decisions and the paths I choose to follow. Ultimately, it is not just about what we achieve; it is about who we become in the process.

Citations:

1. Ford, Henry. *My Life and Work.* New York: Doubleday, Page & Company, 1922, 123.

2. *Steve Jobs*: *"Stanford University Commencement Address,"* June 12, 2005, accessed September 14, 2021, https://news.stanford.edu/2005/06/14/jobs-061505/.

Chapter 9

The Entrepreneur's Evolution

A Dark Cloud Overhead

The years following 2011 were among the most challenging of my life. As an entrepreneur, I have always faced obstacles head-on. Still, nothing could have prepared me for the news that my dear friend Debjit was diagnosed with Langerhans cell histiocytosis (An abnormal clonal proliferation of Langerhans cells, abnormal cells deriving from bone marrow and capable of migrating from skin to lymph nodes), a rare form of cancer. The diagnosis struck like a bolt of lightning, bringing a sudden darkness that seemed to envelop everything. Debjit had become more than just a colleague - he was family. Our lives had become intertwined in ways that went beyond business, and his illness was a blow that affected not just him but all of us who cared deeply for him.

In times of great adversity, people often reveal their true character. Despite the gravity of his diagnosis, Debjit remained resilient. He was determined to fight the disease with everything he had, and I was equally determined to support him in any way possible. We mobilized all the resources we could for his treatment, from surgeries to chemotherapy. Fortunately, his cancer was not the most aggressive kind, but it was a silent killer, lurking in the shadows and striking without warning.

Debjit's battle with cancer was a constant reminder of the fragility of life, but it also underscored the importance of perseverance. As the legendary showman P.T. Barnum once said, *"The show must go on."* And so, even as we navigated this personal crisis, the demands of our business could not be ignored. I had to find a way to balance my responsibilities to the company with my desire to be there for my friend. It was a delicate dance that required emotional resilience and unwavering focus.

During this period, my role as an entrepreneur was tested in ways I had never imagined. Balancing the emotional weight of Debjit's illness with the need to keep the business running was a tightrope walk. During these challenging times, I learned some of the most profound lessons about leadership. Leadership is not just about steering the ship in calm waters; it's about keeping it afloat during the storm. I realized that my role was to manage the business and be the pillar of strength for those who relied on me, including Debjit.

The experience also brought me face-to-face with the reality that life is unpredictable and can change instantly. This realization made me more determined to build something lasting to withstand life's storms. It was this resolve that fueled my next steps as an entrepreneur.

Closing an Old Chapter

Amidst the challenges of Debjit's illness and the growing complexities of our business, I made another difficult decision in 2011 - one that marked the end of an era for me. I decided to close the Ascent Tutorial permanently. Ascent Tutorial had been the cornerstone of my entrepreneurial journey, the foundation upon which I had built my career. It provided me with financial stability, a sense of purpose, and a source of great pride. However, as my training business expanded and demanded more of my time and attention, I found it increasingly difficult to justify my continued engagement in giving tuition.

The decision to close Ascent Tutorial was not an easy one. I knew that it would hurt my financial health temporarily, and it did. The income from Ascent Tutorial had been a significant part of my earnings, and closing it meant a temporary loss of revenue. But I also knew that to focus entirely on the growth of my training business and realize my long-term vision, I needed to let go of the past and embrace the future.

Letting go of Ascent Tutorial was like saying goodbye to an old friend. It had been a reliable source of income and a platform where I honed my teaching skills and built my reputation. But as with all things in life, there comes a time when we must let go of the familiar to embrace new opportunities. The decision to close the tutorial was driven by the understanding that my time and energy were finite resources. I could not expand my training business to its full potential while still being tied to the day-to-day demands of running the tutorial.

In retrospect, the closure of Ascent Tutorial marked the end of one era and the beginning of another. It allowed me to direct all my energy and resources toward expanding the training business, and while the financial impact was immediate, it was also temporary. Within a relatively short period, I recovered the lost income and began earning almost double of what I had made while still being engaged with Ascent Tutorial. This experience reinforced the idea that sometimes, you must be willing to close specific chapters in your life to move forward.

The decision to close Ascent Tutorial also taught me the importance of focus in entrepreneurship. I realized that spreading oneself too thin can be detrimental in long-term success. By focusing on my training business, I could grow it in ways that would not have been possible if I had continued to divide my attention. This valuable lesson would shape my approach to business in the future.

A Vision of Independence

I found myself increasingly at odds with our franchisor during this difficult time. The differences in opinion between us were becoming more pronounced, and I began to feel marginalized. Despite my significant contributions to developing new training programs - programs that went beyond the BPO training that had been the company's sole focus-the directors of the franchisor company failed to acknowledge my efforts. I felt I was outgrowing the confines of the franchise model, and the realization that I was no longer seen as a valued partner led me to consider a new path.

It was the moment when a new idea took root. I envisioned possibly creating my own company that would reflect my values, vision, and approach to business. I wanted to build something truly my own, free from the constraints of a franchisor who seemed increasingly out of touch with my ambitions. The thought was both exhilarating and daunting, but I knew that if I were to achieve the kind of success I envisioned, I would need to take this bold step.

Entrepreneurship is often about recognizing when to strike out on your own. As the saying goes, "If you don't build your dream, someone else will hire you to help build theirs." I had reached a point where I could no longer ignore the growing disconnect between my aspirations and the direction the franchisor was taking. I founded my company because I knew it was the only way to achieve my desired success and fulfilment.

On September 11, 2012, I made my move. I gathered all my senior managers for a meeting and laid out my vision for the future. I proposed starting a new company that would be ours, built from the ground up with the lessons we had learned over the years. The response was overwhelmingly positive. I could see their excitement and anticipation of embarking on a new journey, and I knew we were ready to take on this challenge together.

'Ascensive' was born, ushering in a new era for us. The Ministry of Corporate Affairs (MCA) approval came on December 26, 2012, a date that would forever be etched in my memory as the birth of a new beginning. Despite his ongoing health struggles, Debjit resigned from his position with our franchisor and joined me at Ascensive. His commitment to our latest venture was a testament to his character and our shared vision, even as cancer took its toll on his body.

Starting Ascensive was like stepping into the unknown. We were venturing into uncharted territory, and while the future was uncertain, the potential was limitless. Transitioning from being a franchisee to owning my own company was challenging and liberating. It required me to think differently, approach problems with a new mindset, and take on a level of responsibility I had not experienced before. But with these challenges came opportunities - opportunities to create something truly ours.

The Struggle for Recognition

However, the road ahead was anything but easy. Convincing students to enrol in our new brand was a daunting task. The lack of a proven track record made it difficult to gain their trust, and our initial marketing efforts did not yield the results we had hoped for. The shifting dynamics of the ecosystem compounded the challenges of establishing a new brand in a competitive market. The skill development landscape was evolving rapidly, and we struggled to keep pace.

In these moments of struggle, I often reflected on the words of Steve Jobs: "I'm convinced that about half of what separates the successful entrepreneurs from the non-successful ones is pure perseverance." We were in a position where perseverance was not just a virtue but a necessity. The early days of Ascensive were marked by countless setbacks, from failed marketing campaigns to difficulty securing partnerships. Yet, we met each challenge with determination and a refusal to give up.

During this time, Dr. Pranab Mukherjee led the formation of the National Skill Development Corporation (NSDC). The NSDC was established to promote skill development across India by fostering the creation of large, quality vocational training institutions. It provided funding to enable these centres to reach out to the masses, intending to skill 500 million people by 2022. The formation of the NSDC represented a significant opportunity for us, but despite our best efforts, we could not secure a partnership or funding from the organization.

It was a bitter pill, but it forced me to think creatively. I knew that if we were to survive, we needed to find an alternative way to tap into the opportunities presented by the NSDC. After careful consideration, I decided to reach out to a company that is already an NSDC partner. Over time, I built a relationship with the company's leadership, gradually earning their trust and offering my assistance to help them fulfil their training commitments to the NSDC.

Through this collaboration, I became closer to the company's leaders and eventually confided in them my aspirations of becoming an NSDC partner. They were supportive and offered to help me navigate the complex process of securing a partnership. It was a crucial turning point for us, opening the door to new possibilities and providing us with a roadmap for moving forward.

The struggle for recognition and partnership with the NSDC was a lesson in patience and persistence. It taught me that success is often a matter of timing and that sometimes, the best opportunities come from unexpected places. By aligning ourselves with a company already established in the NSDC ecosystem, we could leverage their expertise and resources to position ourselves for future success.

Seizing the Opportunity

Amid this, the Government of India announced a groundbreaking initiative funding ₹1,000 crores to incentivise skill development under a new STAR (Standard Training Assessment and Reward) scheme. The STAR scheme was designed to encourage skill development by offering monetary rewards to trainees who completed approved training programs. The scheme was a game-changer, providing financial incentives to trainees and training providers making skill development more accessible to the masses.

The announcement of the STAR scheme was a moment of great excitement and hope for us. It was an opportunity to scale our operations and reach a broader audience. But with this opportunity came the challenge of ensuring we could deliver on our promises. The scheme was highly competitive, and only the most effective training providers could secure the funding and support needed to succeed.

With the assistance of the Retailers Association's Skill Council of India in Mumbai, we managed to onboard ourselves into the scheme, positioning our company as an associated partner. Our name and contact details appeared prominently on the NSDC website, signalling our entry into a new era.

To capitalize on this opportunity, I secured funding from private lenders. Debjit, despite his ongoing battle with cancer, led his team with unwavering determination. We drove expansion like never before, onboarding over fifty franchisees quickly. It was as if the stagnant car of our business had finally started running again. The STAR scheme provided us with the desperately needed lifeline, allowing us to generate revenue, gain national recognition, and secure a place in the rapidly evolving skill development landscape.

The success of our involvement in the Star scheme was a testament to the power of seizing opportunities when they arise. It was a reminder that in entrepreneurship, timing is everything. The Star scheme gave us the financial resources we needed to grow and the credibility and recognition we had been striving for.

Reflecting on this period, Howard Schultz's words ring true: 'In times of adversity and change, we truly discover our essence.' Indeed, this was a time of profound adversity, but it was also a time of immense growth. Our challenges forced me to evolve from a hands-on entrepreneur to a strategic manager. I had to integrate the lessons learned from Capacity, Collaboration, and Capital into a cohesive management strategy that could guide us through the complexities of this new business environment.

Emergence of a Strategic Leader

The transformation was about scaling up or expanding our operations and becoming a leader who could inspire others to believe in our vision. I learned to delegate effectively, empowering my team to take ownership of their roles while I focused on steering the company in the right direction. This shift in focus allowed me to see the bigger picture, anticipate market changes, and adapt our strategies accordingly.

One of the most important lessons I learned during this time was the value of resilience. The journey was far from smooth, and there were moments when the challenges seemed insurmountable. Yet, each setback taught me something new about the business, my team, and myself. I realized that authentic leadership is not about avoiding obstacles but about facing them head-on, learning from them, and emerging more substantial on the other side.

Another key lesson was the importance of building a solid foundation. The three Cs-Capacity, Collaboration, and Capital were the pillars upon which Ascensive was built, but it was the M-Management that held everything together. Effective management requires a deep understanding of these elements and the ability to integrate them into a unified strategy. It meant having the right resources and partnerships, knowing how to allocate them effectively, and fostering a culture of collaboration and innovation within the organization.

Building a cohesive team was another crucial aspect of this transformation. As we navigated the challenges of establishing a new brand, the importance of a strong, cohesive team became increasingly evident. Debjit's leadership, even as he battled cancer, was a source of inspiration for everyone in the company. His resilience and commitment demonstrated the power of leading by example, and his influence helped shape the culture of Ascensive. Our team was not just a group of employees; we were a family united by a shared vision and a common goal.

Our success during this period was a testament to our hard work, determination, and validation of our strategic decisions. The partnerships we formed, the risks we took, and the lessons we learned all contributed to the growth and evolution of Ascensive. It was a journey that required constant adaptation, but it was also one that brought us closer to realizing our full potential.

I remained focused on the future as we continued to expand and evolve. I knew the business landscape would continue to change, and I was determined to stay ahead of the curve. The experiences of these years have taught me that growth is not just about scaling up; it is about constantly evolving, about being willing to reinvent oneself and one's business in response to new challenges and opportunities.

By the end of this period, I had established Ascensive as a leading player in the skill development industry and laid the groundwork for its future growth. The journey was far from over, but I was confident we were on the right path. The lessons I had learned, the relationships I had built, and the strategies I had implemented would continue to guide us as we moved forward.

Reflecting on the Journey

Warren Buffett states, *"The difference between successful people and successful people is that successful people say no to almost everything."* This quote resonated with me as I reflected on our decisions during this time. The ability to focus on what mattered to say no to distractions and stay committed to our vision was crucial to our success.

Looking back on this chapter of my life, I am filled with pride and gratitude. The challenges we faced were immense, but so were the rewards. The evolution from an entrepreneur to a strategic manager was not easy, but it was a journey that transformed me in ways I could never have imagined. It taught me the importance of resilience, the power of collaboration, and the value of strategic thinking. It showed me that actual growth is not just about expanding one's business but about evolving as a leader, manager, and person.

This chapter in the story of Ascensive is a testament to the power of perseverance, the strength of collaboration, and the importance of visionary leadership. It is a reminder that, no matter how daunting the challenges may seem, there is always a way forward. And it is an affirmation that anything is possible with the proper foundation, team, and strategy.

Citation:

1. Buffett, Warren, quoted in Alice Schroeder, *The Snowball: Warren Buffett and the Business of Life*. New York: Bantam Books, 2008, 561.

Chapter 10

Long March to Delhi

"Na Hi Kaścit Kṣaṇam Api Jātu Tiṣṭhaty Akarmakṛt;
Kāryate Hy Avaśaḥ Karma Sarvaḥ Prakṛti-Jair Guṇaiḥ"

"न हि कश्चित्क्षणमपि जातु तिष्ठत्यकर्मकृत् ।
कार्यते ह्यवशः कर्म सर्वः प्रकृतिजैर्गुणैः ॥"

"Indeed, no one can ever remain for even a moment without acting; everyone is forced to act helplessly according to the qualities born of material nature. "— Bhagavad Gita 3.5

Capitalising the Opportunity

The successful execution of the Star Scheme was more than just a feather in our cap it was the beginning of a new era, a pivot point that would set the stage for unprecedented growth and innovation in our company. When the Government of India launched the Standard Training Assessment and Reward (Star) Scheme, many training providers saw it as an opportunity to make money. They focused on churning out trainees, completing assessments, and claiming government incentives with little regard for the actual impact on the students' lives.

We decided to take a different path, driven by a philosophy rooted in actual value creation rather than mere financial gain. Our approach was simple yet revolutionary: students would pay the course fees upfront and only receive the government's monetary reward upon completing their training and subsequent placement. This method was against the prevailing trend, where most providers handed out free training and banking on government payouts alone.

The beginning was tough. Convincing students to pay upfront in an ecosystem where free training was the norm was challenging. However, we believe in the long-term benefits of our approach. We knew that students who had already invested in their education would be more committed, translating into better training outcomes and higher placement rates. It was an uphill battle that we were prepared to fight.

As the days passed, we began to see the fruits of our labour. Our placement rates were significantly higher than our competitors, and word began to spread about the quality of our training programs. The government monetary reward was no longer the main draw; the assurance of quality education and guaranteed placement brought students to us.

A Wrong Number: A Right Relationship

One incident during this period stands out as a turning point, underscoring the importance of persistence, luck, and human connection. My team faced issues with batch creation in the NSDC's (National Skill Development Corporation) system, which was crucial for processing our training assessments and ensuring timely government rewards for our students. We tried contacting the concerned official multiple times, but the phone kept ringing. Frustrated by the lack of response, my team asked me for help.

I decided to give it one last try, dialling an arbitrary extension number in the NSDC office, hoping to reach someone who could assist. To my surprise, the call was answered by a man who switched to speaking Bengali - my mother tongue after hearing my name and company details. The conversation quickly transformed from a formal query to a warm, engaging dialogue.

The man on the other end was Kaushik, a senior official at NSDC.

Kaushik's immediate connection with me wasn't just because of our shared language but because of his genuine interest in our work and challenges. He listened attentively to my concerns and immediately offered helpful solutions. More importantly, Kaushik became a mentor and a guiding light in the complex labyrinth of government regulations and processes. His advice and support became invaluable as we navigated the bureaucratic maze often accompanying large-scale government projects.

Our relationship with Kaushik soon transcended the professional realm. He became an elder brotherly figure, someone I could rely on for professional and personal advice. His guidance was instrumental in helping us grow, and our bond only strengthened with time.

One day, during one of his official visits to our branch, Kaushik proposed something that felt like a dream come true. Impressed by the outcomes of our training programs and the meticulous way we executed the Star Scheme, he suggested that we consider becoming an official partner of NSDC. The idea of being an NSDC partner was akin to reaching for the moon - an opportunity that seemed distant and unattainable just months before.

Seizing the Moon

The idea of becoming an NSDC partner was electrifying. It wasn't just about the prestige; it was about the opportunity to expand our reach, scale our operations, and solidify our position as a leader in skill development. However, the road to partnership was not going to be easy. The requirements were stringent, the competition fierce, and the stakes higher than ever.

But with Kaushik's encouragement and my team's unwavering dedication, we decided to go for it. The process was rigorous. We had to fulfil numerous criteria, submit detailed proposals, and demonstrate our capability to manage large-scale training programs across multiple states. We also needed significant capital to support the expansion, and this is where our innovative approach to capital management came into play.

One of the key lessons I had learned over the years was the importance of blending Capacity, Collaboration, and Capital what I often referred to as the three Cs of entrepreneurship. It was the moment to put those lessons into practice. We meticulously planned our financial strategy, ensuring we could meet the investment requirements without compromising our operational integrity.

After months of preparation, we finally signed the partnership agreement with NSDC. The project outlay was nearly ₹4 crores, of which NSDC provided 70% as debt with a mere 6% annual interest rate. It was a massive win for us, both financially and strategically. We now had the backing of the government and the resources to scale our operations across ten significant states in India.

Expanding Horizons: Scaling Across India

With the NSDC partnership secured, we were ready to expand our footprint nationwide. We established a new office in the heart of the city - a hub that would serve as the command centre for our operations. From this new headquarters, we coordinated our activities across different states, ensuring that our training programs were delivered consistently and with the highest quality standards.

This period was marked by rapid growth. Our revenue and profits tripled within a few years, making us one of the key players in the skill development ecosystem. We began receiving government projects nationwide, further solidifying our position in the market.

The expansion was not without its challenges. Managing operations across ten states required coordination and efficiency that we had never experienced before. It was during this time that my management capacity was truly tested. I had to rely on my team more than ever, delegating responsibilities and empowering them to make decisions.

The collaborative nature of our organization became our greatest strength. My team members Pranamya, Debasish, Soumitra, Saptarshi, Kamalesh and Sandip were not just employees but partners in our journey. Their commitment to the company's vision and ability to work together as a cohesive unit were instrumental in overcoming the many hurdles we faced.

One of the most rewarding aspects of this period was seeing the growth of my team members. They, too, were evolving, developing new skills, and taking on greater responsibilities. This growth was a testament to the culture of collaboration we had cultivated over the years a culture where every member was encouraged to contribute, innovate, and lead.

Innovation was at the heart of our success during this period. We didn't just focus on scaling our existing operations; we constantly sought new opportunities, markets, and ways of doing things. I realized innovation wasn't just about creating new products or services but about thinking differently, challenging the status quo, and finding creative solutions to complex problems.

One of the most significant innovations we introduced was a new business model that differentiated us from other training providers. While most companies were focused solely on government-funded programs, we began exploring the possibility of creating hybrid models that combined government support with private funding. This approach allowed us to diversify our revenue streams and reduce our dependence on any single source of income.

We also invested heavily in technology, integrating digital tools into our training programs to enhance their effectiveness. It improved our students' learning experience and allowed us to scale our operations more efficiently. Technology became a key differentiator for us, enabling us to deliver high-quality training to students in even the most remote parts of the country.

Another area where we innovated was in our approach to partnerships. We actively sought collaborations with other organizations within and outside the skill development sector. These partnerships allowed us to leverage the strengths of our collaborators, bringing in new expertise and resources that complemented our own.

One of our most successful partnerships was with a technology company specialising in e-learning platforms. This partnership enabled us to offer online training programs, reaching a broader audience and allowing our students to learn independently. The success of this initiative was a clear example of how collaboration and innovation could create new opportunities and drive growth.

Team Resilience: Key to Success

As our company grew, so did the need for a robust and professional team. My collaborative nature and capacity in the field attracted many talented individuals, many of whom had previously worked with my former franchisor. These individuals brought a wealth of experience and knowledge, and their contributions were instrumental in taking our company to new heights.

One of the most significant aspects of this period was the development of our team's capacity. We invested heavily in training and development, ensuring our team members had the skills and knowledge to excel in their roles. This investment paid off in spades, as our team members met and often exceeded their expectations.

The collaborative spirit within our organization was evident in everything we did. We worked together to solve problems, to overcome challenges, and to seize new opportunities. This sense of unity was a crucial factor in our success, and it created a work environment where everyone felt valued and motivated.

Our team's expansion allowed us to take on larger, more complex projects. The NSDC partnership, for example, required a level of coordination and expertise that would have been impossible without the right team in place. Our success in executing these projects was a testament to the strength and resilience of our team.

The Road Ahead

As we continued to grow, we faced our fair share of challenges. The rapidly changing market dynamics and the increasing complexity of our operations meant that we had to adapt and evolve constantly. Despite the challenges, we remained determined and focused on finding solutions.

One of the most significant challenges we faced was managing our growth while maintaining the quality of our training programs. Expanding into new regions required us to maintain consistent standards everywhere. It required meticulous planning, constant monitoring, and a willingness to make tough decisions when necessary.

Another challenge was the increasing competition in the skill development sector. As more companies entered the market, we had to find ways to differentiate ourselves and maintain our competitive edge. It was where our focus on innovation and collaboration truly paid off. By constantly seeking out new opportunities and exploring new ways of doing things, we were able to stay ahead of the curve and continue our growth trajectory.

However, the onset of the COVID-19 pandemic in 2020 brought new challenges that tested our business's foundations. The pandemic disrupted our operations, halted our expansion plans, and got us face-to-face with the possibility of failure. It was a time of uncertainty, and the future of our company hung in the balance.

But even in the face of such adversity, we remained resilient. The management capacity we had built over the years, combined with the collaborative spirit of our team, enabled us to navigate the challenges posed by the pandemic. We adapted our operations, explored new opportunities, and continued to push forward, even when the odds seemed insurmountable.

From Follower to Leadership

As I reflect on this period of our journey, I am reminded of a quote by Steve Jobs: "*Innovation distinguishes between a leader and a follower.*"[2] This quote encapsulates the essence of what we achieved during this time. Through innovation, collaboration, and a relentless pursuit of growth, we were able to transform our company into a leader in the skill development sector.

The lessons we learned during this time were invaluable. We know that innovation is not just about creating new products or services; it's about finding new ways to think, solve problems, and seize opportunities. We learned that collaboration is the key to unlocking new possibilities and that by working together, we can achieve far more than we could ever achieve alone.

We also learned the importance of resilience the ability to keep pushing forward, even in adversity. This resilience was built on solid management, a commitment to our values, and a belief in the power of innovation.

As we move forward, these lessons will continue to guide us. The journey is far from over, and undoubtedly, more challenges are ahead. But with the foundation we have built, the team we have assembled, and the lessons we have learned, I am confident that we will continue to grow, innovate, and explore new opportunities.

Citations:

1. Ford, Henry. *My Life and Work.* New York: Doubleday, Page & Company, 1922, 123.

2. *Steve Jobs: "Stanford University Commencement Address,"* June 12, 2005, accessed September 14, 2021, https://news.stanford.edu/2005/06/14/jobs-061505/.

Chapter 11

Believer of the Dream

"The future belongs to those who believe in the beauty of their dreams." – Eleanor Roosevelt

The Onset of a New Challenge

The world drastically changed in 2020, leaving a lasting impression on our memories. The onset of COVID-19 was unexpected, and like many others, I was initially unaware of the gravity of the situation. The first few days of the lockdown felt strangely relaxing a forced break that allowed me to spend more time with my family, engage in evening prayers, watch movies, and even focus on my health with regular exercise. Slowing down and enjoying life's simple pleasures was a rare opportunity.

However, as the days turned into weeks, the initial sense of calm gave way to growing concern. The uncertainty of when or if things would return to normal began to weigh heavily on my mind. The lockdown, which had initially felt like a temporary pause, started to seem more like a long-term disruption. My thoughts shifted from enjoying the present to worrying about the future - both for my family and business.

A Story that Shook Me to My Core

During these uncertain times, I received a message from a friend, KG, who had once been a business rival but had since become one of my closest allies. The message contained a story that profoundly impacted me - a story that would become a guiding light during one of the most challenging periods of my life.

The story was about Lord Indra and the farmers. Upset with the farmers, Lord Indra announced that there would be no rain for 12 years, effectively dooming their crops. The farmers begged for pardon, and Lord Indra told them that rain would only come if Lord Shiva played his Damru, knowing that he had secretly asked Lord Shiva not to agree to the farmers' request. When the farmers approached Lord Shiva, he repeated Indra's words and told them he would play his Damru only after 12 years.

Disheartened, most farmers decided to wait out the 12 years, but one farmer continued to dig, treat, and put manure in the soil. He sowed seeds regularly, even though he knew no crops would emerge. The other farmers ridiculed him, asking why he was wasting his time and energy when he knew the rains wouldn't come.

The farmer's reply was simple: "I know that crops won't come out, but I'm doing this as a matter of practice. Even after 12 years, I might forget how to grow crops and work in the field. I need to keep doing it to stay in shape and prepare for the next rainy season.

Goddess Parvati praised the farmer's wisdom and warned Lord Shiva that even he could lose the ability to play the Damru after 12 years. Anxious, Lord Shiva decided to try playing the Damru right then, and as soon as its sound filled the air, rain began to pour down. The farmer who had kept practising saw his crops emerge immediately, while the others were disappointed.

The story's moral was clear: "The game is won during the practice, not during the performance. If you are waiting for the right opportunity to start practising, you have already lost the race." This story shook me to my core, serving as a potent reminder that even in the most challenging times, it is crucial to keep pushing forward, practising, and staying prepared when the opportunity finally arrives.

Adapting to the New Normal

Inspired by this story, I knew I had to take immediate action to keep my business afloat and my team motivated. The lockdown had shut down our physical training centres, and with government payments delayed, our capital was dwindling. We couldn't continue as before the situation demanded innovation and adaptability.

I organised an online meeting with my entire team, and for the first time since the lockdown began, we came together to discuss our situation and brainstorm possible solutions. The atmosphere was tense; everyone was concerned about the future and the safety of their loved ones. But despite the fear and uncertainty, there was also a shared determination to find a way forward.

We decided that laying off employees was not an option. Instead, we cut allowances temporarily, ensuring everyone could still make a living. Our focus shifted to creating online courses—a far more complex task than we initially imagined. This new venture required the Q&A team, the training delivery team, the sales team, and our IT vendors to work together closely.

The process was gruelling, involving endless meetings, countless hours of planning, and a steep learning curve for everyone involved. But the story KG had sent me kept playing, reminding me that this was our practice that the work we were doing now would prepare us for the future, even if the results weren't immediately visible.

As we launched our online courses, the initial response was slow. We were competing in a crowded digital marketplace, and it wasn't easy to stand out. But slowly, our efforts began to pay off. Our students appreciated the quality and accessibility of the courses, and word began to spread. It wasn't the same as running our physical centres, but it was a lifeline that kept us going during those dark days.

The Struggle for Survival

Despite our best efforts, the financial strain was immense. Every day was a battle to keep the business running - to pay our employees, to meet our obligations, and to find ways to generate revenue. I began travelling, even within the restrictions of the lockdown, to collect long overdue payments. In some cases, I was successful, but it was never enough to stabilise our finances fully.

The stress was overwhelming. I could feel the weight of the situation bearing down on me, threatening to crush the optimism and drive that had always been my strengths. There were moments when I thought this might be the end - not just of my business but of everything we had worked so hard to build.

But in those darkest moments, I remembered the farmer who kept practising, and I realised that these challenges were building something within me - something more robust, more resilient. Bad days are not bad at all, I told myself. They are opportunities to build capacity, withstand adversity, and prepare for even more significant challenges. In these moments of struggle, our experiences help us discover our potential and become who we are meant to be.

Initiating to Going Public

Amid the chaos and uncertainty, an idea began to take root—one that harkened back to my earlier days in the stock market. In 2008, when I ran a sub-agency for a stockbroker, I observed how companies grew by accessing public funds. Those experiences taught me valuable lessons about the capital markets that shaped my understanding and stayed with me even as I transitioned to skill development and training.

The COVID-19 pandemic rekindled that interest. As I watched the markets fluctuate wildly, I saw an opportunity - a chance to take my company public and raise the capital needed to survive the pandemic and thrive in its aftermath. The government promoted the SME exchange, a platform for startups to access public funds. It was a new frontier, and I was determined to explore it.

However, nearly everyone around me met the idea with scepticism. Publicising a company was complex and risky, especially during a global pandemic. But I was undeterred. The challenges of the past few months reinforced my belief in the power of perseverance, and I knew that this was the right move for the future of my company.

I began the painstaking process of preparing for the SME exchange. It involved navigating a maze of regulations, preparing financial statements, and ensuring our business was in the best shape to attract investors. It was an enormous undertaking that required focus, dedication, and a deep understanding of our strengths and vulnerabilities.

I kept my team informed and involved as I worked through the process. I wanted to understand not just the "what" and "how" of our strategy but the "why." It was more than just a business decision; it was a commitment to the future of our company and everyone who was a part of it. I needed them to share my vision and believe in what we could achieve together.

During this time, I realised what our external and internal challenges were. The success of publicising the company would depend not just on my vision but on the strength and resilience of our entire team. We needed to work together more closely than ever before, to support each other through the difficult moments, and to celebrate the small victories along the way.

I encouraged my team to see this as an opportunity for growth not just for the company but for themselves as individuals. We invested in professional development, providing training and resources to help them build new skills and adapt to the rapidly changing business landscape. I wanted them to feel empowered, know their contributions were valued, and understand that they were integral to our success.

As the months passed, the bonds within our team grew more vigorous. We were no longer just colleagues but a family united by a common purpose. This sense of collaboration was a powerful force that enabled us to overcome obstacles that seemed impossible.

One of the most significant lessons I learned during this period was the importance of empathy and communication. The pandemic had taken a toll on everyone, and it was crucial to acknowledge that and create a space where people felt safe to express their concerns and fears. By fostering a culture of open communication and mutual support, we could navigate the pandemic's challenges with solidarity and shared responsibility.

The Light at the End of the Tunnel

By the end of 2020, our efforts were beginning to bear fruit. We had successfully transitioned many of our training programs online, trying our best to secure funding through the SME exchange. We were starting to see signs of recovery in our financials. The journey had been incredibly challenging, but it had also been transformative.

Looking back, I can see how the experiences of this period prepared us for the future. The pandemic forced us to innovate, to think creatively, and to adapt quickly to a rapidly changing environment. It also reinforced the importance of the three Cs - Capacity, Collaboration, and Capital - essential to our survival and thriving during this time.

Capacity: We built new skills, individually and as a team, that enabled us to navigate the challenges of the pandemic. We developed online training programs, mastered new technologies, and found innovative solutions to complex problems.

Collaboration: We strengthened our relationships within our team and with external partners. The sense of unity and shared purpose that emerged during this time was a powerful force that helped us overcome the many obstacles we faced.

Capital: We secured the necessary funding in the coming time to support our operations and fuel our growth. The decision to take the company public was bold, but it gave us the resources to continue our journey.

I am filled with optimism and confidence as we look to the future. The past years challenges have tested us in ways we could never have anticipated, but they have also made us more robust, resilient, and prepared us for whatever lies ahead. We have emerged from this crisis with a renewed sense of purpose and a clear vision for the future.

In the next chapter, I will share how we successfully navigated the process of publicising the company - a journey filled with challenges and triumphs. But for now, I am grateful for the lessons learned, the bonds forged, and the opportunities ahead. The future is bright, and I am excited to see where this journey will take us next.

Chapter 12

Capitalising the Capital Market

"Success is not final, failure is not fatal: It is the courage to continue that count." – Winston Churchill.

Landing on Stock Exchange

Taking my company public was a dream I had carried for many years. It symbolised success and the culmination of everything I had worked toward as an entrepreneur. However, the path to this goal was far from straightforward. As anyone who has navigated the process of listing a company will tell you, it's a journey full of complexities legal requirements, compliance with regulatory frameworks, financial disclosures, and the challenge of convincing investors that your company is worth backing.

Yet, despite these hurdles, I was determined to push forward. The decision to go public wasn't just about securing more capital for the business; it was about creating lasting value for my company and the community we served. The journey to public success was not just mine it belonged to every individual who had worked alongside me over the years, contributing to our shared vision of growth and impact.

This chapter marks the realisation of that long-held goal. It wasn't a solo achievement, and it wasn't a straightforward one. It resulted from collective effort, perseverance, and a strategic approach to overcoming challenges.

The Pillars of Support

I wouldn't have achieved this milestone without the unwavering support of four key pillars: my merchant banker, Prerna (my student-turned-CFO), the accounts team comprising Shilpa and Sandip, and my executive assistant, Pranamya. Each of them brought a unique skill set and commitment to the table, and together, we worked relentlessly to make the public listing a reality.

The Merchant Banker: A Brother in Arms

Our merchant banker played a pivotal role in guiding us through the intricacies of the IPO process. Initially, he was a financial expert brought on board to help us navigate the maze of capital markets and regulatory frameworks. But over time, he became more than that he became a younger brother to me, a trusted advisor who always had my back.

His deep market sentiment knowledge and ability to connect us with the right investors were invaluable. He helped demystify many of the complexities of the public listing process, ensuring we were always ahead. But more than his professional expertise, his support made the difference. Whenever I doubted whether we would succeed, he was there to remind me of the strength of our company and the value we were bringing to the market.

Prerna: From Student to CFO

Prerna's journey from being one of my students to becoming the Chief Financial Officer of our company is a story that fills me with pride. Her dedication and brilliance were apparent even in her youth, and witnessing her rise to a leadership position in our company has been a highlight of my entrepreneurial journey.

As CFO, Prerna ensured that our financials were in perfect order. The public listing required transparency, precision, and compliance with many regulations areas where Prerna excelled.

She worked tirelessly, collaborating with auditors and legal teams, to ensure we met every requirement without a hitch. Her attention to detail and commitment to excellence were critical to our success.

Prerna's leadership in managing the financial disclosures gave me the confidence that we were presenting our company in the best possible light. It wasn't just about numbers; it was about showcasing the value we had built over the years and convincing investors that we were a company worth betting on.

The Accounts Team: Shilpa and Sandip

A dedicated team led by Shilpa and Sandip ensured the meticulous management of details behind every significant financial undertaking. Their invaluable leadership in the company's daily financial operations was instrumental in positioning us for the IPO.

They worked long hours, often sacrificing weekends and holidays, to ensure everything was in place. Whether managing internal audits, handling regulatory filings, or preparing detailed financial reports, Shilpa and Sandip were relentless in their pursuit of accuracy. Without their efforts, meeting the deadlines and maintaining the high standards required for a successful listing, this would have been impossible.

Pranamya: My Right Hand

My executive assistant, Pranamya, was another essential player in this journey. From coordinating investor meetings to managing my schedule and ensuring every detail was accounted for, he played an instrumental role in keeping the entire process on track.

His ability to multitask and handle the logistics of the listing process freed me up to focus on the bigger picture. He was always one step ahead, anticipating problems before they arose and ensuring the team worked harmoniously. In many ways, he was the glue that held everything together during the most intense moments of the journey.

The Challenges of Listing During a Pandemic

As if the complexities of going public weren't enough, we faced additional challenges with the onset of the third wave of the COVID-19 pandemic. Movement restrictions, financial uncertainty, and general market unpredictability added to the pressure we were already facing.

There were moments of doubt when I wondered whether the timing was right, whether investors would see the value in our company, and whether we could pull this off during such uncertain times. However, the confidence I had built over 16 years of being an entrepreneur gave me the strength to move forward. The capacity we had developed as a team, along with the collaborative spirit that defined our work culture, enabled us to keep pushing ahead.

Despite the obstacles, we managed to conduct successful investor connect programs. We communicated our vision for the company, shared our growth strategy, and provided detailed insights into our financial health. These meetings were about selling our company, building trust, and demonstrating the value we had created over the years.

A Moment of Triumph

On the 12th of January, Swami Vivekananda's birth anniversary, we launched our IPO - a day that will forever be etched in my memory. The event took place in the iconic Great Eastern Hotel in Kolkata, a venue steeped in history and grandeur, which mirrored the significance of the moment for me and my family.

As I stood there, the mixture of emotions were overwhelming excitement, anxiety, and the hope that the market would validate years of hard work. The air was thick with anticipation as we awaited the response from investors. Swamiji's words, "Arise, awake, and stop not till the goal is reached," resonated within me, reminding me of the journey that had brought us here.

As the news came in, the response was better than I had imagined-our IPO was oversubscribed four times. Investors saw the value and potential we had built. The outburst of emotion from my parents was something I will never forget. They had witnessed my journey from the beginning, and seeing their pride and tears of joy made the success even more meaningful.

It wasn't just a personal victory but a shared triumph for my team, our investors, and my family. The event at the Great Eastern Hotel marked the realization of a long-cherished dream, paving the way for a future filled with new possibilities.

Reflections and Looking Ahead

Reflecting on the journey of taking the company public, I am filled with a deep sense of gratitude and pride. This milestone culminated after years of hard work, strategic planning, and the unwavering belief that we could achieve something remarkable.

But I am also keenly aware that this is just the beginning. The journey of entrepreneurship is a never-ending way. Each milestone represents not just an ending but a new beginning. Taking the company public was a dream realised, but there are still more challenges to face, more goals to achieve, and more opportunities to explore.

The process of going public taught me invaluable lessons—about perseverance, the importance of teamwork, and the power of strategic thinking. It also reinforced the significance of the three Cs: Capacity, Collaboration, and Capital. These elements are indispensable to our achievements and will continue to steer our path forward.

A Milestone Reached

As I close this chapter, I realise how far we've come and how much further we still have to go. Achieving public success was a milestone that I will always cherish, but it is only one part of the more extensive journey. New challenges are ahead, new markets to explore, and new goals to set.

For now, I am content to reflect on what we have achieved. I am deeply grateful for the support of my team, our investors, and everyone who believed in our vision. The next chapter of our journey will be filled with new challenges and opportunities, but I am confident we are ready to face them.

As I conclude this book, I am already thinking about the next one the story of the new challenges we faced, the lessons we learned, and the victories we celebrated after achieving public success. But for now, I will take a moment to appreciate the journey so far, knowing that the best is yet to come.

Citations

1. Churchill, Winston. *Never Give In: The Best of Winston Churchill's Speeches.* London: Pimlico, 2003, 42.

2. *Steve Jobs: "Stanford University Commencement Address,"* June 12, 2005, accessed September 14, 2021, https://news.stanford.edu/2005/06/14/jobs-061505/.

3. Ford, Henry. *My Life and Work.* New York: Doubleday, Page & Company, 1922, 123.

Epilogue

The Entrepreneur's Theory of Relativity

karmaṇy-evādhikāras te mā phaleṣhu kadāchana
mā karma-phala-hetur bhūr mā te saṅgo 'stvakarmaṇi

"कर्मण्येवाधिकारस्ते मा फलेषु कदाचन ।
मा कर्मफलहेतुर्भूर्मा ते सङ्गोऽस्त्वकर्मणि ॥"

"You have a right to perform your prescribed duties, but you are not entitled to the fruits of your actions." - Bhagavad Gita, Chapter 2, Verse 47

As I sit down to pen the final words of this book, I reflect on the journey that brought me here, not just as an entrepreneur but as someone who has learned to view business and life itself through the lens of relativity. This journey, with its countless highs and lows, has made me realise that entrepreneurship is far more complex than it seems on the surface. It isn't merely about profits and losses, expansion and contraction, or success and failure. It is a continuous balancing act, much like the universe itself.

I named this book *E=MC³: The Entrepreneur's Theory of Relativity*. The title isn't just a metaphor; it encapsulates the essence of the entrepreneurial journey. Much like Einstein's theory of relativity, which revealed how space and time are interconnected and dependent on the observer; entrepreneurship is a dynamic equation that requires mastery of multiple variables working together in harmony.

In my equation, *E* stands for the Entrepreneur, the driving force behind every venture. The Entrepreneur is the nucleus, holding everything together, balancing ambition, innovation, and resilience. Just as energy in Einstein's theory represents the power to move and transform, similarly does the Entrepreneur embody the energy that pushes an idea into reality. But energy alone is not enough. In business, this energy must be carefully harnessed and directed.

That's where *M* comes in *Management*. The importance of management cannot be overstated. It is the discipline that transforms raw energy into sustainable action. It is not simply about overseeing operations but guiding an entire ecosystem, understanding that each decision ripples through the organisation's fabric, just as gravitational waves ripple through space-time. Management provides structure, a framework within which creativity and risk-taking can thrive.

And then, there are the three Cs - *Capacity, Collaboration, and Capital* - the variables that drive growth and sustainability.

- *Capacity* is the Entrepreneur's ability to learn, grow, and adapt. Entrepreneurs must continuously build capacity within themselves and their team in a rapidly changing world. The lessons I've learned from adversity have expanded my capacity in ways I could never have anticipated.

- *Collaboration* is the recognition that no journey is made alone. Whether it was the partnerships that helped us grow or the team that stood by me through the most challenging moments, collaboration has always been the engine of our progress; just as in physics, where the interaction of forces creates momentum, collaboration in business accelerates growth.

- *Capital* represents the lifeblood of any business-the resources necessary to turn vision into reality. But capital isn't just financial; it includes intellectual and social capital, the relationships and knowledge that empower entrepreneurs to weather storms and seize opportunities.

This framework - *E=MC³* - is not just a catchy title; it's a formula that has guided me through every challenge, every decision, and every triumph. It is a reminder that, much like in Einstein's universe, everything in business is relative interconnected, dynamic, and dependent on the forces around it. To succeed as an entrepreneur is to understand and navigate these relationships, to find the balance between ambition and limitation, innovation and tradition, and risk and reward.

As I look back on the milestones we've achieved, culminating in the public listing of our company, I see this theory of relativity in action. Going public was not just a financial transaction; it was the convergence of years of growth, struggle, and collaboration. It was the realisation of a dream that had been years in the making, shaped by the forces of Capacity, Collaboration, and Capital, each playing a crucial role in our success.

Yet, just as in science, no theory is ever truly complete. There is always more to learn, more to explore. The process of listing the company was an achievement, but it was also the beginning of a new chapter one that promises new challenges, new opportunities, and new lessons. I've learned that an entrepreneur's journey never truly ends; it evolves like the expanding universe.

As I conclude this book, I realise that the path of entrepreneurship is a continuous dance of forces, just like the theory of relativity describes the dance of matter and energy. The Entrepreneur must remain adaptable, open to change, and aware that success, like the universe, is in constant motion.

The lessons and stories I've shared are one chapter in an ongoing saga. More challenges, more milestones to reach, and, undoubtedly, more complex decisions will be ahead. But the formula remains the same: $E=MC^3$. It is a theory I will carry forward with me, and I hope it serves as a guide for anyone who embarks on their entrepreneurial journey.

In closing, I leave you with another verse, one that has guided me through the many highs and lows of my journey:

"Uddhared Atmanātmānaṁ Nātmānam Avasādayet;
Atmāiva Hyātmano Bandhur Atmāiva Ripur Atmanaḥ"

"उद्धरेदात्मनात्मानं नात्मानमवसादयेत् ।
आत्मैव ह्यात्मनो बन्धुरात्मैव रिपुरात्मनः ॥"

"One must elevate, not degrade, oneself by one's mind. The mind alone is the friend, and the mind alone is the enemy of the self." - Bhagavad Gita, Chapter 6, Verse 5

The mind of the Entrepreneur is the true battleground. It can be your greatest ally, propelling you toward success, or your most significant obstacle, holding you back in fear and doubt. Choose wisely, and may your journey, like mine, be one of growth, resilience, and the relentless pursuit of your dreams.